# Charlie Watts

Printed and bound in Great Britain by MPG Books Ltd, Bodmin

Distributed in the US by Publishers Group West

Published by Sanctuary Publishing Limited, Sanctuary House, 45–53 Sinclair Road, London W14 0NS, United Kingdom

www.sanctuarypublishing.com

ISBN: 1-86074-581-4

# Charlie Watts

Alan Clayson

**Sanctuary**

*To Alan Barwise*

'It is better to have a permanent income
than to be fascinating'
*Oscar Wilde*

# Contents

# About The Author

Born in Dover, England, in 1951, Alan Clayson lives near Henley-on-Thames with his wife, Inese, and sons, Jack and Harry. His portrayal in the *Western Morning News* as 'the AJP Taylor of the pop world' is supported by *Q*'s 'his knowledge of the period is unparalleled and he's always unerringly accurate'. He has written many books on music, including best-sellers *Backbeat* (subject of a major film) and *The Yardbirds*, as well as for journals as diverse as *The Guardian*, *Record Collector*, *Mojo*, *The Times*, *Mediaeval World*, *Eastern Eye*, *Folk Roots*, *Guitar*, *Hello!*, the *Independent*, *Ugly Things* and, as a teenager, the notorious *Schoolkids' Oz*. He has also performed and lectured on both sides of the Atlantic, as well as broadcast on national TV and radio.

From 1975 to 1985, he led the legendary group Clayson And The Argonauts and was thrust to 'a premier position on rock's Lunatic Fringe' (*Melody Maker*). As shown by the formation of a US fan club – dating from a 1992 soirée in Chicago – Alan Clayson's following has continued to grow, as has demand for his talents as a record producer and the number of cover versions of his compositions by such diverse acts as Dave Berry – in whose Cruisers he played keyboards in the mid-1980s – and New Age outfit Stairway. He has also worked with The Portsmouth Sinfonia, Wreckless Eric, Twinkle, The Yardbirds, The Pretty Things and the late Screaming Lord Sutch, among others. While his stage act defies succinct description, he is spearheading an English form of *chanson*. Moreover, his latest album, *Soirée*, may stand as his artistic apotheosis, were it not for the promise of surprises yet to come.

Further information is obtainable from www.alanclayson.com.

# Prologue
## Onlooker

'Charlie was a very hermit-like guy. His mind always seemed to be somewhere else. He didn't seem to join in the flow of it at all.'

*– Michael Putland, Rolling Stones photographer* [1]

His membership of The Rolling Stones will always remain central to any consideration of Charlie Watts as a figure in time's fabric. Nevertheless, he was often a mere onlooker, a bit-part player at most, during many of the more conspicuous events that have punctuated the group's four decades as one of the showbusiness sensations of the past century. Neither has he ever commented much either on, say, the drugs busts that all but destroyed the Stones in the late 1960s; the crisis at Altamont that threatened to ruin their reputation, the business in Canada with the prime minister's wife... Therefore, I make no apologies for telescoping these and other episodes for literary and chronological convenience.

Moreover, as George Harrison had been categorised for all time as the 'Quiet Beatle' in 1963 – with Ringo Starr a close second – so some pressured journalist chronicling the mayhem surrounding The Rolling Stones in 1964, came up with 'the Silent Stone' as a description for Charlie. This phrase stuck, fuelled as it was by media frustration at his reluctant and, seemingly, bored utterances in interviews and when a stick-mic was thrust at his mouth every time the Stones had been through customs at an airport.

He opened up to specialist outlets in the 1980s after he'd formed the first of several critically acclaimed amalgams to indulge his abiding passion for jazz, but, until then, Watts provided little 'good copy' beyond raw information and bald aphorisms such as the oft-quoted, 'A career in rock 'n' roll comprises five years playing and twenty years hanging about.'[2]

Not surprisingly, it was without much hope that I attempted to elicit Charlie's assistance with this biography. He did not deign to reply to my letter assuring him that mine was to be a respectful account, concentrating mainly on his professional career and artistic output, that it would not peter out after the swinging '60s, that I was not some scum reporter, but an *artiste* like himself. I wanted him to like it. His silence was galling, but a recent biographer of William Rufus hadn't spoken to his subject either, and there was far more information available about Charlie than about William, much of it from press archives and conversations with many of those with whom Watts and his Rolling Stones were associated.

For most of my research concerning modern drumming and insight into Charlie Watts' impact on same, I went first and last to Alan Barwise, drummer and philosopher with Billy And The Conquerors, Clayson And The Argonauts and other ventures, quixotic and otherwise, which I have instigated over the past 30-very-odd years.

Please put your hands together, too, for Iain MacGregor, Laura Brudenell, Rachel Holmes, Dicken Goodwin, Albert DePetrillo, Michael Wilson, Kathleen Meengs and, particularly, Chris Harvey for patience and understanding about a deadline that I almost-but-not-quite met.

Thanks are also in order for Pat Andrews, Dave Berry, Don Craine, Keith Grant-Evans, Phil May, Dick Taylor and Twinkle for their candour and intelligent argument.

Whether they were aware of providing assistance or not, let's have a round of applause, too, for these musicians: Roger

Barnes, Peter Barton, Cliff Bennett, Clem Cattini, Mike Cooper, Tony Dangerfield, the late Lonnie Donegan, Chris Gore, 'Wreckless' Eric Goulden, Brian Hinton, Robb Johnston, Garry Jones, Graham Larkbey, Tom McGuiness, Brian Poole, Jim Simpson, John Steel, Mike and Anja Stax, the late Lord David Sutch, John Townsend, Paul Tucker and Pete York – plus three cheers for Carlo Little, former Cyril Davies All-Star, Lord Sutch Savage and – just – Rolling Stone.

It may be obvious to the reader that I have received help from sources that prefer not to be mentioned. Nevertheless, I wish to thank them, as well as Robert Cross of Bemish Business Machines, Stuart and Kathryn Booth, Peter Doggett, Ian Drummond, Katy Foster-Moore, Richard Hattrell, Michael Heatley, Dave Humphries, Rob Johnstone, Allan Jones, Mick and Sarah Jones, Iris Little, Elisabeth McCrae, Russell Newmark, Mike Ober, Mike Robinson, Hilary Stafford-Clark, Anna Taylor, Michael Towers, Warren Walters, Gina Way and Ted Woodings, and of course Inese, Jack and Harry Clayson for suffering by proxy the cruel and unusual personal traumas I endured during the writing of this book.

*Alan Clayson*
*February 2004*

# 1 Drums

'A good drummer who swings makes everybody else play
better.'

*– Don Hyman*[1]

He'd finish 1964 neck and neck with Dave Clark as the second
most famous drummer in the world. The first, of course, was
Ringo Starr – and like The Beatles' most junior partner, Charlie
Watts had been sucked into a vortex of events that hadn't
belonged even to speculation when he came to consciousness in
a city neighbourhood that unfurled on to the mud banks of a
working river.

Charles Robert Watts had entered the world in Islington's
University College Hospital on 2 June 1941, the overcast and
unseasonably cool day that clothes rationing was introduced to
help the country pay for the downfall of Hitler. Until well into the
1950s, a meal with chicken was a rare treat – though the Welfare
State was to provide *gratis* third-pint bottles of lukewarm milk for
morning break at school. Yet some items would be so scarce that
you could only buy them with weeks of saved-up ration coupons.

Another so-called stop-gap measure was the construction
between 1945 and 1949 of nearly 200,000 lookalike 'prefab'
homes to accommodate young families. The assembly of a single
such estate of small, unprepossessing bungalows could take less
than a fortnight, but some proved more enduring than the more
permanent housing promised by the government as soon as post-
war labour could be mobilised.

'As much thought has been put into this plan as was put into the invasion of North Africa,' enthused Prime Minister Churchill, who didn't have to live in a prefab as Charlie and his sister Linda would with mother Lilian and father Charles Richard, a lorry driver for British Rail's parcels division. From the cradle, the children caught and held a Cockney accent, but theirs was not a *cor blimey* environment of pubs, back streets, 'ello-'ello-'ello policemen and sub-criminal adult dialogue revolving around booze, dog racing and dodges for making easy money – as portrayed in *The Blue Lamp*, *Passport To Pimlico* and similar black-and-white Ealing Studios output.

While Charlie remembered the prefab as 'tiny but very cosy',[2] it was situated on the edge of pasture in rural London – not quite the contradiction in terms it might seem in the capital's present-day austere and functional aesthetic of tower blocks and right-angled grids of inner distribution roads. Indeed, as Charlie observed half a century later, the district where he'd grown up had 'gone back to fields again now – which is very unusual'.[2]

In 1948, however, the family moved to Kingsbury, as much Middlesex as London, where the patches of green were not farmland, but country parks, sports grounds and play areas within earshot of the North Circular Road and, more so, the clattering national and internal railway connections across a lugubrious suburb that was becoming indistinguishable to outsiders from any other on the north-western fringes of the metropolis.

By the time he started at Tyler's Croft Secondary Modern four years later, Charlie's upbringing had been as undramatic and free from major calamities as that of any seemingly ordinary bloke who could 'give the impression of being bored, but I'm not really. I've just got an incredibly boring face.'[3] Just above middle height with brown hair and blue-grey eyes, he was as self-effacing about his abilities at school where he was recognised as a talented soccer player who preferred cricket. His ambidextrous bowling was impressive enough to gain him a try-out for the

Middlesex county club. He also won trophies for sprinting. Less laudable was Charlie's skill, apparently, at settling playground altercations with his fists as much as reasoned argument – an inclination that would rear up in heated moments during his adult life too. At Tyler's Croft, he may have been in the mood for a fight after physical education – because 'What I hated were the gym classes: all that drag about getting changed, and leaping and running and jumping. I mean, it didn't get you anywhere.'[4]

Similarly, while he proved to be sound academically too – with end-of-term prizes for Art and English – he didn't join the school choir or do particularly well at music, which was then taught as a kind of mathematics whereby a dotted crotchet, say, was expressed diagrammatically by 'three of the little milk bottles you have at school'.[5]

Neither were 'musical evenings' of any description a frequent occurrence – if they ever occurred at all – in the Watts household, even before television became an indispensable domestic fixture. 'I reckon the only instrument any of them could play at home was the gramophone,' laughed Charlie.[4] Yet music started to become central to his life from around the age of 11.

It began with the BBC Light Programme's diet of pre-rock 'n' roll pop aimed principally at children and, especially, the over-30s. There was little middle ground between 'How Much Is That Doggie In The Window' and 'Love And Marriage'. Now and then there'd be lewd outrages like 'Such A Night' by Johnnie Ray, 'the Prince of Wails', but otherwise you jumped from nursery rhymes to Frank Sinatra as if the intervening years were spent in a cultural coma.

The radio music that most captivated the adolescent Watts was the kind that bordered on jazz. When the tip of classic rock's iceberg was sighted, he found the white executants less impressive than their black counterparts, but was otherwise 'of the school that never listened to rock 'n' roll – or refused to until I was about twenty-one. I never followed the charts.'[2]

He was, however, very taken with 1952's million-selling 'Flamingo' by saxophonist Earl Bostic, former sideman with drummer Lionel Hampton, who had emerged from the big bands of the 'swing era' that was petering out after the war. Within months of hearing 'Flamingo', Charlie's imagination had been captured by jazz as surely as Don Quixote's had by the windmills of Castile. 'I never had any trouble listening to it,' he explained. 'It's very easy for me.'[2]

The spiral into dependency became breakneck. He came to love all its roots and branches – ragtime, traditional, mainstream, modern, avant-garde, 'cool', 'hot', New Orleans, Kansas City, New York, Chicago – whether the orchestral euphoria of Duke Ellington and Count Basie, the white swing of Benny Goodman and Woody Herman – for whom Stravinsky composed *Ebony Concerto* – vocal dare-devils such as Sinatra, Buddy Greco, Billy Eckstine and Anita O'Day and, when he was able to obtain them on import, the differing textural complexities of Ornette Coleman and Roland Kirk. Charlie travelled too the vinyl road to the 'hard bop' of The Jazz Messengers and, inevitably, freeform via the 'be-bop'[6] – or just plain 'bop' – of John Coltrane, Charlie Mingus, Thelonius Monk, Dizzy Gillespie, Miles Davis – and, above all, alto saxophonist Charlie 'Yardbird' Parker. Indeed, so far as Charlie Watts ever had a boyhood hero, it was the late Parker he admired as other lads might footballer Stanley Matthews – 'the Wizard of Dribble' – or champion boxer Freddie Mills.

How do such interests start? How about yours? Was it because your first remotely romantic encounter – a chaperoned kiss under the mistletoe – was soundtracked by *Session With The Dave Clark Five*? Perhaps a teacher on whom you had a crush supported Sheffield Wednesday. Charlie Watts has never revealed whether any specific incident or person turned him on to the endlessly inventive Parker, only that, 'He sort of epitomised an era in my life. Even now, although I may only play him once a month, I still get that good feeling.'[7]

As well as listening to what was in the grooves of the discs, Watts became preoccupied with their creators, seeking insights into artistic conduct, clarification of obscurer melodic – and, if relevant, lyrical – byways, and generally searching for information about what made the musicians tick. He wished for the impossible: 'I'd like to have gone to the Savoy Ballroom – Chick Webb, I think. I'd love to have seen Ellington at the Cotton Club and have dressed up for the occasion. I'd love to have seen Charlie Parker at the Royal Roost or something like that...Louis Armstrong, probably at the Roseland Ballroom in Chicago in the 1930s with a big band behind him...'.[8]

The nearest he could get was reading reminiscences about the old days when *dramatis personae* – some from the form's ragtime dawn – were interviewed on the jazz pages of *Melody Maker* or in *Downbeat*, the US jazz periodical – and by listening to the records over and over again, sometimes focusing on maybe only the piano or bass, then just the horns. Furthermore, while he enjoyed the tactile sensation of handling the packagings of *The Duke Plays Ellington*, *The Benny Goodman Story Volume One*, *Charlie Parker Plays Cole Porter* and more of the new plastic 10- or 12-inch 33$\frac{1}{3}$ rpm long players – LPs – he also made myriad private observations while learning much from sleeve notes, composing credits and listings of personnel. This often led him to the canons of associated players. Having invested that amount of cash – the equivalent of a fortnight's newspaper-round earnings for every LP – Charlie intended to get his money's worth.

Perhaps the most singular road-to-Damascus moment was when the 14-year-old heard 'Walkin' Shoes', a 1956 instrumental of 'cool' persuasion by The Gerry Mulligan Quartet. If a little 'Light Programme' to the undiscerning ear, and with saxophone and trumpet solos to the fore, Charlie homed in on the scuffed snare and tom-tom propulsion of Chico Hamilton, 'the first guy that I ever heard on record that made me want to play the drums'. [2] As a result, he began concentrating less on Ellington, Goodman, Parker, Davis, Monk *et al* than on a particular fellow wielding the sticks behind them on their respective LPs: 'Kenny Clarke is probably my favourite drummer. No one had a touch like him, especially on cymbals. It was a float, a touch that he invented.[9] I would have been about fifteen when I first heard him, and that would have been the Charlie Parker stuff. He did four tracks with Parker. One of the faults of listening to great players is that you know you could never accomplish that.'[2]

Rather than being particularly thrilled by drum solos, Watts came to realise that while it was, say, a trumpeter or saxophonist who gave a number its outward shape and direction, it was often the drummer that made the truest difference – and that the best of them did not merely maintain a precise backbeat, but lifted a band off the runway, allowing it to glide easily on the strongest musical winds.

Chico Hamilton notwithstanding, Charlie's first drumming idol was Joe Morello – 'all taste and elegance'[8] – best known to the man in the street for accompanying Dave Brubeck, one of the few modern jazz pianists to reach the pop charts without compromising his stylistic determination.[10] Nevertheless, everyone who sat at the head of the table in the Valhalla of North American jazz percussion was worthy of the attention of a young man half a world away.

Off-the-cuff examples are Count Basie's most renowned drummer, 'Papa' Jo Jones – despite his hurling an angry cymbal at Charlie Parker's high-velocity blowing in which the tune had been lost – hunchbacked Chick Webb, whose orchestra once rivalled Goodman's; Roy Haynes who was with both Coltrane and Kirk; audacious Philly Jo Jones, dragging and accelerating the beat behind Miles Davis; Big Sid Catlett – as enthralling on brushes as he was with sticks – Earl Palmer and snappy dresser Shelly Manne, omnipresent in the recording studios of Hollywood; Chicago's Dave Tough from Woody Herman's first Herd, who planted successful feet in both the swing and be-bop camps – Mingus's Dannie Richmond – 'The rhythms would turn inside each other – because Mingus would make it do that'[11] – and Art Blakey. A master of dynamics, Blakey could create, gasped Charlie, 'deafening noise and then he'd come down, and your breathing would be louder than his playing, but there'd be no let up in the intensity'.[2] Blakey's Jazz Messengers were to be the flagship act of Blue Note, a US jazz record label of such prestige that hearts would pound in anticipation at the sight of its logo in a rack at Dobell's, the jazz specialist shop along London's Charing Cross Road.

Successive editions of *Downbeat* also sold well at Dobell's. Charlie saw Max Roach, the most adventurous of all early be-bop drummers, in all his glory on the front page of a special drumming issue in 1956. Without breaking sweat, Roach could drum like a rhythmically integrated octopus. 'Maybe only another drummer can understand exactly what he is doing and how well he does it,' thought Watts, 'but I can listen to a brilliant drummer for hours on end.'[4]

In doing so, he appreciated rather than liked band leader Buddy Rich – every smart alec's notion of percussive splendour – and Gene Krupa, such a jazz legend that he was to be the subject of a 1960 bio-pic: 'Everything he did was exaggerated. Every move was a big deal – but he was one of the best.'[7]

Therefore, in reveries that no one could penetrate, Charlie Watts was not Rich or Krupa commanding the stage alone under his own voodoo spell for minutes on end, but ministering unobtrusively to overall effect behind a genius like Parker.

He decided to put action over daydreaming. Other boys might have gone no further than smiting the furniture to music from the radio, but Charlie began exploring avenues with wider implications than inadvertently annoying houseproud parents. Apart from rattling about on biscuit tins (with Cadbury's Roses giving the most authentic snare drum sound), the cheapest option was a Viceroy 'tapbox', advertised in the *New Musical Express*, with miniature drum, washboard, cowbell and hooter that, for 39s 11d, was 'ideal for parties and playing with radio or gramophone'. There was also a Broadway 'Kat' snare-and-cymbal set costing £10/4s.

Impressed by neither, Charlie pondered. Somehow or other, he'd acquired a banjo, but during cursory attempts to teach himself to play, 'couldn't get the dots on the frets right. It drove me up the wall.'[7] One day, he removed the strings and the connecting screw to the neck, and was left with an object with metal rim, vellum skin and resonator. It was an approximation of a small snare drum.

After constructing a stand from a Meccano set, he bought a pair of not sticks, but wire brushes – because those were what Chico Hamilton had used for the subtleties of 'Walkin' Shoes'. As Charlie's consequent rhythmic experiments in his bedroom neither disturbed the rest of the household nor interfered with school, Mr Watts didn't object to his son's hobby. Indeed, that Christmas, he gave Charlie a basic second-hand kit – bass drum, snare and cymbal – of indeterminate make[12] – though he and Lilian realised swiftly that it was 'the worst thing you can get a kid. They're an awful lot of fun, but the worst instrument to actually learn to play, noise-wise. They've got all these practice pad-type things, but there's no point in playing them because half the fun when you first start is the sound of the drums – and the noise is unbelievable. That's part of the horror of playing them – controlling the volume.'[11]

Surprisingly, the neighbours were tolerant – 'a boys-will-be-boys kind of thing,' reckoned Charlie[4] – when, initially, he attacked his present with gusto, showing no signs of ever stopping. Fortunately for them, Charlie absorbed quickly the signals from Art Blakey: 'One of the great things with drums is to be able to play quietly.'[2] As the New Year got under way, his strivings brought forth hand-and-foot co-ordination, accurate time-keeping, a clean roll faster than *moderato*, and the beginnings of an impactive personal style.

There were instructional manuals available, but he couldn't read standard music script, and drum tutors were few and far between then, even in Greater London – so Charlie gathered what he could by trial and error when playing along to records – 'which I hated. It seemed so synthetic'[11] – and through watching other drummers either on television or at the local palais where, in stiff evening dress, the bands helped shut out the staider verities of rationing; newlywed couples having to start married life in one set of in-laws' homes, and front doors slammed on the pervading smell of soiled nappies and over-cooked cabbage.

During the night's veletas, cha-cha-chas and concessions to short-lived fads like the Jitterbug and the Creep, there was always some young dingbat requesting 'Rock Around The Clock', but otherwise 'There wasn't any British rock 'n' roll for Charlie to copy,' notes Alan Barwise, 'so he was forced to be more creative. His backbeat came from using a traditional military marching band grip with, for example, the fulcrum on his left hand between the thumb and forefinger, but right inside the grip. He also had his snare drum in an unusually high position. If it hadn't been like that, he might have lost that loose jazz feel of his.'

While drumming overshadowed the rest of Charlie's adolescence, there were other interests such as the Wild West, which he researched beneath its Roy Rogers-and-Trigger veneer, and maintained an abiding interest into adulthood – particularly in the US Civil War. He was an avid listener to radio comedy – where his tastes ran to *Hancock's Half Hour* rather than the more off-beat *Goon Show*. He was also given to drawing cartoons supplemented with fragments of verse and prose.

This was reflective of his flair for art – as was the embossing of his initials on his bass drum skin and, crucially, the fluttering of a General Certificate of Education 'O' level pass in the subject on to the Watts doormat in August 1957. This, plus a favourable testimonial from Tyler's Croft, was enough to gain him a place on a three-year course at Harrow School of Art, beginning the following month. Thus the world of work could be kept at arm's length for a while longer, enabling the fancy that he'd like to make a living as a musician to enter Charlie's index of possibilities.

'Musician', see, no longer meant sitting in the fourth row of violins and cranking out Beethoven all your life or, indeed, conforming to any school dictates about what was and wasn't 'decent' music. You didn't even have to be born into showbusiness any more. Admittedly, jazz didn't coin much, but, like Shelly Manne did, you could finance such a combo if you got to know the right people and were sufficiently versatile and coldly professional to take on studio session work in the employ of whoever called the shots, with no extra time or favours done. You could also get a foot in the door via servitude under the batons of middle-aged band leaders on luxury liners and at debutante balls.

Charlie was well placed to pursue such paths as the British music business was centred, then as now, in London – as was the British take on skiffle. Specifically, it was traceable to a metropolitan jazz band led by trombonist Chris Barber. Most of its repertoire consisted of 'Bill Bailey', 'High Society' – both issued as singles – and further set-works from the ragtime portfolios of Louis Armstrong, Kid Ory, Sophie Tucker *et al* – though clarinettist Monty Sunshine's style, for example, was derived as much from the European *klezmer* form of lower-register improvisation as any toot-tooting from New Orleans, and it was significant that The Dutch Swing College Band, Germany's Old Merrytale Jazz Band and other pre-eminent traditional jazz outfits *sur le continent* absorbed their music from British 'dads' like Sunshine and Barber rather than its US originators.

On his band's 1954 LP, *New Orleans Joys*, Barber allowed singing banjo player Lonnie Donegan a crack at 'Rock Island Line', one of two 'skiffle' novelties amid the interweaving intensity of the front line that dominated the remaining tracks. There were sufficient Light Programme airings of 'Rock Island Line' to warrant its issue as a spin-off 78 in autumn 1955. Its climb into the Top 20 in both Britain and the United States made it expedient for 24-year-old Donegan to go solo – though an understanding Barber promised him his old job back when it was all over. This gratifying turn of events was milked with two high-profile US tours, but though Lonnie's skiffle was derived from the rent parties, speakeasies and Dust Bowl jug bands of the US Depression, 'rockabilly', its closest relation in primeval rowdiness, gripped the American teen infinitely tighter.

Nevertheless, on figuring out the same three bedrock guitar chords, his Limey cousin could (and generally did) form a skiffle ensemble with friends. Aspirant skifflers would be everywhere, stretching out limited repertoires at wedding receptions, youth clubs, church fêtes, birthday parties and every talent contest advertised.

As well as an embarrassment of slashed acoustic guitars, at the core of its contagious backbeat were tea-chest-and-broomstick bass, a washboard tapped with thimbles, dustbin-lid cymbals, biscuit-tin snare drum and further vehicles of musical effect fashioned from everyday implements. Like punk after it, anyone could try skiffle – and the more ingenuous the sound, the better. The highest ideal was to forge an individual style by making even 'Rock Island Line' *not* sound like any other outfit's version.

Soon, those skifflers who meant business were running up hire purchase debts for the amplified guitars and orthodox dance band drum kits that were to supersede the finger-lacerating acoustic six-strings and pots-and-pans percussion that were becoming old hat during interval slots for jazz bands at Ken Colyer's Studio 51, London's oldest jazz club, not to mention fuller sessions down in the Heaven And Hell, Le Macabre, the Safari and, deepest in the heart of Soho, the 2 I's, all-skiffle basements within the square mile bordered by the consumer's paradises of Park Lane, Piccadilly, Shaftesbury Avenue, Charing Cross Road and Oxford Street.

Yet, though it was known that Lonnie Donegan had drummed with a jazz band when on National Service – and that mere ownership of a kit attracted offers for your services all over a given area – Charlie Watts' ventures into skiffle were irresolute. David Green, a next-door neighbour – and lifelong friend – had manufactured a tea-chest bass, but the two never progressed much further than talking about starting up a group. They spent more hours spinning discs in one or other's bedroom before skiffle lost its flavour on the bedpost overnight, and Charlie started at art school.

# 2 Art

'I'd be off in the corner, talking about Kirkegaard. I always took myself seriously, and thought Buddy Holly was a great joke.'

*– Charlie Watts* [1]

Within Harrow School of Art's imposing white-stone edifice, Charlie completed an all-purpose foundation course before specialising in graphics and lettering. He also absorbed a hidden curriculum via a restless and omnivorous debauch of reading during which his understanding of which books were worthwhile and which were not became more acute. His brow might have furrowed over Soren Kirkegaard, the Danish mystic, and certain of his existentialist descendants, chiefly Jean-Paul Sartre, but he was less enraptured with the US connection, epitomised by Jack Kerouac and William Burroughs, foremost prose writers of the 'Beat Generation', and associated bards such as Corso, Ginsberg and Ferglinghetti.

Initially, he was disinclined to air his learning, extra-curricular and otherwise, during college tutorials. Indeed, for much of his first terms there, Watts said as little as possible, and tended to walk alone. Yet he began to fix on details that most others in a given lesson might be too lackadaisical to consider or even notice. He seemed also to be more *au fait* with the historical traditions and conventions of art and its interrelated philosophies than they.

Perceived as slightly eccentric, he distanced himself further by not conforming to the unofficial art student – and 'beatnik' –

uniform of army-surplus duffel coat draped with a long scarf, polo- or turtle-neck pullover down to the knees, sandals or desert boots, a CND badge and corduroy trousers that looked as if they'd hung round the legs of a particularly disgusting builder's labourer for the past three years. Had the wearers got round to actually reading Molière they might have quoted, *Guenille, si l'on veut: ma guenille m'est chère* – Rags they may be: my rags are dear to me. In the toilets, male collegians with beards that hadn't quite taken would examine themselves in the mirror. They were letting their hair grow long, and hoped it was beginning to show.

Charlie, however, modelled his appearance on that of Shelly Manne, a vision of sartorial and depilatory understatement in the pages of *Downbeat*. Family approval of this choice was attested in Linda cutting her brother's hair as regularly as he wished, and her father offering advice about and paying for Charlie's conservative and narrow-lapelled suits and shirts with button-down collars – 'and I wore them as smartly as I could. I didn't like jeans and sweaters in those days. I thought they looked untidy, and didn't feel somehow as good as I did in my suits with the baggy trousers.'[2]

He was, however, at one with beatnik friends at college in his taste in music. Ostensibly snooty about pop, even as a nod to Dada and then Pop Art's mannered revelling in junk culture, someone throwing a *demi-monde* party – usually when his or her parents were away – ensured that the artless scattering of LPs surrounding the record player were the coolest modern jazz. Guests might also be treated to glimpses of unconscious comedy during 'impromptu' in-person musical entertainment involving, maybe, scat-singing, bongo-tapping and a saxophone honking inanely.

At student union shindigs, other exhibitionists would don boaters or top hats, and a variety of hacked-about formal wear, drink heavily of cider, and launch into vigorous steps that blended a type of skip-jiving with the Charleston in a curious galumphing motion to the plinking and puffing of an outfit trading in traditional jazz – 'trad' – during a post-skiffle craze bracketed roughly by international best-seller 'Petite Fleur' in 1959 – attributed to Chris Barber and his Jazz Band, but, essentially, a clarinet solo – and the same combo framing the ebullient singing of Ottilie Patterson, Barber's then-wife, over the closing credits of 1962's *It's Trad Dad* movie.

It had started gaining ground ten years earlier, and an explanation of how by Lonnie Donegan, one of the movement's central figures before his ennoblement as 'King of Skiffle', is worth quoting at length: 'By the time I was demobbed, The Crane River Jazz Band had formed in Cranford, Middlesex, with Ken Colyer on trumpet, and Monty Sunshine on clarinet. They were the first band to get that authentic New Orleans feel. Ken joined the merchant navy just so that he could jump ship in New Orleans to worship at the Holy Grail. Had he not done that, British pop would not be what it is today. We owe it all to Ken Colyer – because he brought back so much invaluable experience, information and contacts.

'In the interim, Monty had led The Crane River Jazz Band, and my own jazz outfit was coming on in leaps and bounds. Chris Barber had a band too, which wasn't great shakes – though he was. All of us used to get together at the Prince Alfred at Mile End, at weekends, and play all night long. From this emerged the first professional English jazz band, named after Chris. We shot off to Denmark for six weeks so no one here would hear us in the rough, and played every night for whatever we could get to keep alive. When we got back, we gained a residency at the London Jazz Club in the Crypt at Marble Arch. Our first gig was a triumph, and it went from there.'

Yet it was not London but Bristol, where clarinettist Bernard 'Acker' Bilk was king, from which the pestilence of trad was to ravage Britain to the detriment of rock 'n' roll and fast-fading skiffle. It would spread beyond the earnest obsession of the collegiate intellectual fringe and 'Ban The Bomb' marches to a proletariat where 'ACKER' was studded on the backs of leather jackets where 'ELVIS' once was, and girls fainted to the blowing of Humphrey Lyttelton, Kenny Ball, Sunshine, Barber and Bilk. After the latter came within an ace of a Number One with 'Stranger On The Shore' a Manchester disciple wrote to ask him if it was about Jesus Christ.[3]

It was pop by any other name – as were Top Ten strikes by The Temperance Seven, jazz only marginally but still booked for television programmes like the BBC's opportunist *Trad Tavern*, and at jazz strongholds such as the 100 Club along Oxford Street in central London, Uncle Bonnie's Chinese Jazz Club (!) in Brighton, and Liverpool's Cavern – which, to cater for modern jazz enthusiasts, became 'The Club Perdido' every Thursday.

'Modern' was more Charlie Watts' bag than trad, as demonstrated by his dropping of buzz-words like 'Coltrane', 'Monk', 'Brubeck' and, of course, 'Parker' into conversations in the refectory. Some knew who he meant – particularly by 'Brubeck', poised to be to 'modern' what chart-busting Acker Bilk was to trad. Another symptom of this trend was a minor hit in 1958, 'Topsy Part Two', a 45 based on a 1930s standard and focused on a solo by Cozy Cole, a drummer who'd been with Benny Goodman before the war.

Cole stood on the sidelines of a Top 30 in which other jazz and swing band percussionists – among them Earl Palmer – were also twirling their sticks gratuitously on discs that sounded suspiciously like rock 'n' roll – in which subtle cross-rhythms and dotted 'be-bop' crotchets on the ride cymbal had no place. After breathing the air round Shelly Manne, younger fellow Californian Sandy Nelson's hits – notably 'Teenbeat' and 'Let It Be Drums' – were pared down to monotonous beat against a menacing guitar *ostinato*. He even had the nerve to thus refashion Krupa's 'Big Noise From Winnetka'. From the audience at the Royal Festival Hall, Johnny Dankworth, a dean of British jazz, voiced his dismay through cupped hands when Lionel Hampton jumped on the bandwagon too.

Lapsed UK jazz drummers like Tony Crombie and Rory Blackwell were also socking a crude but powerful off-beat less like that of Bill Haley And The Comets – whose 'Rock Around The Clock' rim-shots were actually quite tricky – than those of Louis Jordan, Bill Doggett, Big Joe Turner and other late 1940s rhythm & blues exponents – possibly so that their gold-digging could be justified because of the blues content in jazz – and vice versa.[4]

With no such pretensions, Tony Meehan from Cliff Richard's backing quartet The Drifters – afterwards The Shadows – tore a page from Sandy Nelson's book with LP tracks like 'See You In My Drums'. A protégé of Rory Blackwell, Jimmy Nicol, a former drum repairer, toured with his own New Orleans Rockers, who tried to please most of the people by walking an uneasy line between rock 'n' roll and trad.

These examples may help to illustrate that the same equation as that linking Elvis Presley to Cliff Richard existed between British and US jazzers – that is, you'd never beat the Yanks, but you could have fun and even make a little money displaying your inferiority complex. Some were more interested in the 'money' aspect than others. Denis Payton, saxophonist with The Dave Clark Five – soon to break attendance records at Tottenham's Royal Ballroom with a repertoire drawn principally from the Top 20 and classic rock – had once been in The Mike Jones Combo, a jazz quartet that Clark was, supposedly, managing.

Burnley's Bobby Elliott – who kept scrapbooks of US jazz drummers as Charlie Watts did back-numbers of *Downbeat* – could tell a similar tale. With cymbals positioned carefully horizontal like Buddy Rich's, he'd splattered patterns and accents across bar-lines in a trio with a weekly residency at Nelson's Rawtenstall jazz club, which also accommodated distinguished visitors from London like Dankworth, Harold McNair – and Don Rendell, who offered Elliott a job as his permanent drummer, but 'maybe even then I knew jazz was a minority sport. You'd get eighty people on a good night. Then I'd play a Saturday afternoon rock session down the Nelson Imperial Ballroom, and there'd be seven hundred and all these girls, and I'd think, "Hang on. I'm no fool." You'd hear Earl Palmer on the early Little Richard stuff. Well, that's drumming for me.'[5]

Pete Morgan, likewise, forsook Oxford's Climax Jazz Band for what became The Fourbeats 'after much heart-searching arithmetic'.[6] Other jazz drummers who also yielded to such temptation included Newcastle's John Steel, who 'drifted into working men's clubs and any sort of stuff like that I could get – and then eventually I got into supper-club work in a resident trio with bow ties, playing "Fly Me To The Moon".' Back in Middlesex, Mickey Waller threw in his lot with The Flee-Rekkers, shortly to slip into 1960's Top 30 with a rocked-up version of 'Greensleeves'.

Though he was still holding down a 'proper' job, Mickey was far ahead of Charlie Watts, whose first public engagements were with a so-so semi-professional unit whose principal stock-in-trade was Jewish wedding receptions. 'I never knew what the hell was going on,' confessed Charlie, 'as I'm not Jewish. What you really need on those jobs is a good piano player. If the piano player's daft, you've got no chance. I don't care if you're Max Roach, you'll only last half-an-hour.'[7]

He was now beating a composite kit consisting of two tom-toms, snare and bass drum with ride and crash cymbals. While he couldn't afford to be fussy, his nose would be glued to the windows of the musical equipment shops dotted around Denmark Street, London's Tin Pan Alley. While these displayed Premier, Carlton and other British kits, he gazed with deeper yearning at *Drumbeat* advertisements for Gretsch, the make most closely associated with the foremost US modern jazz drummers (as well as DJ Fontana, who played with Elvis Presley). Smaller and more compact kits than those employed in most big bands, they were targeted at the quieter be-bop groups, attracted too by Gretsch's warm, wooden tone.

Even if he'd had the money, Charlie couldn't have bought a Gretsch anyway as any type of US drum could not be imported into the country then, owing to government embargoes to protect Premier, Carlton *et al*. Though Tony Meehan had acquired a Gretsch, it was to remain an impossible dream for Charlie until he was nearly 30 when, under less extraordinary circumstances, he might have been secure as a graphic designer. This was certainly the most obvious career option while music remained a mere pastime in which, 'I just used to play with anyone really, which was mostly jazz people, but not on a very high musical level, not the best – though some of them turned out to be the best as time passed.'[1]

Yet his parents weren't the sort to grumble about Charlie wasting his time instead of devoting more of it to his college work. 'I don't know if they were supportive of jazz,' he'd recall, 'but they were certainly supportive of me playing. My dad used to take me to gigs in the car and pick me up. I used to spend everything on taxis because I don't drive. David Green and I used to go on the bus sometimes. We joined a swing band together, and David went on to work at Ronnie Scott's. At the age of eighteen, he was in the house band.'[5]

Charlie was pleased for his bass-playing friend as Ronnie Scott's had been defying all comers as London's principal jazz venue since its opening in 1959 in Soho. For lads from Kingsbury, this quarter of the capital was quite exotic, with its bistros, strip clubs and, lacing the air, the aroma of percolated coffee and mega-tar French cigarettes. Yet, from being a shrine of British pop, the 2 I's now had the tell-tale signs of having known better days with its yellowing photo montage of Tommy Steele, Cliff Richard, Marty Wilde and lesser lights who probably hadn't been near the place since gaining their respective recording contracts as would-be English Presleys. In the ascendant was the open-all-night Flamingo where prototype Mods, even back in 1959, would recognise each other by their clean, short-haired pseudo-suavity and classless, whim-conscious dress sense.

It was flattery of a kind that Watts and Green were accepted not as suburban striplings barely old enough to quaff a cherryade on the premises, but as just two of the crowd when they first ventured into a Flamingo all-nighter. The headlining act was Georgie Fame And The Blue Flames – anticipating 'jazz-rock' by a decade – but Charlie was more captivated by the jazzier supporting quintet who were led by a certain Phil Seaman, 'the best drummer in England. He used to play timpani style – very unusual in those days – but he played with his fingers like a real timpanist. In those days, he was the nearest thing we had to Philly Joe Jones or somebody like that. I learnt to play by watching Phil Seaman play a bass drum or Red Reece, in Georgie Fame's band, play a backbeat.[5]

Another enthralled by Seaman was Peter 'Ginger' Baker, who was from the same part of London as Charlie and David. If skeletal in appearance, he had drummed for Acker Bilk, and was rated as 'bloody good' by Watts, who'd discovered Baker in 'one of the best – well, the most exciting, if not the best – jazz groups in London'.[8]

The Johnny Burch Octet also contained tenor saxophonist Dick Heckstall-Smith, by day an X-ray technician at St Bartholomew's Hospital; Graham Bond, a former Don Rendell sideman, on alto saxophone and keyboards – and, with no way of knowing to what extent his and Charlie Watts' lives were to interweave, Jack Bruce, whose inherited talent had been formalised by his musician parents during a childhood in which he attended no fewer than 12 primary schools in Scotland and North America before the family settled in Glasgow. As a teenager, Bruce's membership of a local choir and his skill as a pianist and cellist facilitated enrolment at the Royal Scottish Academy of Music.

During the skiffle era, he plucked bass lines on his cello in one such combo before purchasing the double-bass that gained him work on the Scottish club and ballroom circuit with The Freddie Riley Trio. Next, he toured Italy with The Murray Campbell Big Band – whose stage attire embraced kilts and clan tartans – before room was found for him in The Scottsville Jazzmen via the simple expedient of firing the incumbent bass player.

After an early evening booking in Cambridge, Bruce caught an *ad hoc* jazz ensemble put together by Heckstall-Smith and Baker for a May Ball at one of the university's colleges. His breath taken away, he insisted on sitting in with them. Bemused by the 19-year-old's apparent arrogance, the group pitched into its most complex arrangements, but Bruce coped admirably. When he was enlisted consequently into the Burch ensemble, rubbing his chin in the audience one night was Alexis Korner, a singing guitarist who'd just been sacked from Chris Barber's band, and was on the lookout for musicians for a new outfit on which he had already bestowed a name: Blues Incorporated.

# 3 Blues

*'I'm part Turk, part Greek and part Austrian, and, as I don't know any part Turk, part Greek and part Austrian music, I feel I'm perfectly entitled to play blues.'*

*– Alexis Korner*[1]

During 1960's exceptionally rainy summer, Charlie switched smoothly from art school[2] to a lowly post at Charles Hobson and Gray, one of numerous London advertising agencies that had sprung up since the war. The wage was sufficient – after his mother's housekeeping cut – to pay for clothes, records and drum accessories. Furthermore, after he'd been shown the ropes, Charlie's flair as a commercial artist pushed him up the ladder within months from tea boy to 'visualiser' in the design studio. He was even to be trusted with an assignment that took him to Denmark for a few winter weeks.

Outside office hours, he still tinkered with cartoons, and was in the process of creating *Ode To A High-Flying Bird*, an articulation of sorts of what was now his worship of Charlie Parker. No other word would do. Charlie Watts worshipped Charlie Parker, and had no particular desire to see the *Ode* published, even if any commissioning editor was interested in, ostensibly, a children's picture book with 'all of Parker's life in it, all wrapped round this fictitious bird'.[3]

Most of his spare time, however, was dominated by drumming. In Denmark, Watts would sit at an unfamiliar kit behind fast US saxophonist Don Byas, who bridged swing and

be-bop. Back home, he had moved on from parochial Jewish
wedding celebrations to an outfit in artistic debt to Thelonius
Monk – which meant that 19-year-old Charlie could – in his
imagination anyway – tap a Gretsch just like Kenny Clarke. The
most regular source of work was Saturday nights at the
Troubadour, an Earl's Court coffee bar that presented both folk
and jazz.

One summer night, Alexis Korner insinuated his way on to
the stage with the group. Still seeking personnel for Blues
Incorporated, he wondered afterwards about Charlie Watts for
whom he had been, in the first instance, an irritation: 'This
man came in wearing Rupert Bear trousers and carrying an
amplifier, which he put above my head. It was only six inches
square, hardly an amp at all, but I still hated it. I thought,
bloody hell – noise!'[4]

A fortnight later, Charlie was in Scandinavia – where 'I sort
of lost touch with things'[5] – but several written and verbal
messages from Korner, requesting his services, reached the Watts
family home. On returning, Charlie sought the learned advice of
a local musician, Andy Wren, pianist intermittently with
Harrow's Screaming Lord Sutch and his Horde Of Savages,
whose first bookings the previous spring had brought instant
national notoriety after Sunday newspapers and a BBC
documentary team focused on their alarming front man's pre-
Rolling Stones long hair – briefly dyed green. It mentioned, too,
the leopard-skin loincloth, woad, bull horns, monster feet,
collapsible cage, caveman's club, the inevitable coffin and
whatever else he'd laid his hands on in a tireless effort to elicit
publicity. The music was almost an afterthought, but a maiden
single, 'Big Black Coffin' – retitled, advisedly, 'Til The Following
Night' – was pending.

Wren – who, modelling himself on Ray Charles, also sang
with the nascent Blues Incorporated, urged Watts to take up
Korner's offer. Another deciding factor was that members of the

formidable Johnny Burch Octet had also been enlisted to assist Alexis and Blues Incorporated's subordinate co-founder, Cyril Davies, another vocalist – and a far stricter blues purist than Korner – who also blew the mouth organ, an instrument Charlie had hitherto associated more with the theme to the BBC television series *Dixon Of Dock Green*.

Nevertheless, Watts was to perceive Cyril's 'God-given talent'[4] as well as learn that he – like the less versatile Korner – cut a familiar figure as a session musician in metropolitan studios when not attending to his panel-beating business in South Harrow. It may have occurred to Charlie then that Blues Incorporated could be a useful shop window for a talented drummer too – particularly as a recording contract for the band with Decca, one of Britain's biggest labels, was a foregone conclusion, according to Alexis.

Living hundreds of miles further than Watts from the core of UK pop, Bobby Elliott had distinguished himself in a shortlist – that included a lively sticksman from Wembley named Keith Moon – to fill the drum stool with The Fentones, who backed Shane Fenton, resident vocalist on *Saturday Club*, the Light Programme's principal pop showcase.

Other of Charlie's percussive contemporaries were going onwards and upwards too. Having taught himself to read the relevant dots, Jimmy Nicol was now in the ranks of David Ede And The Rabin Rock, Light Programme regulars, whose upbeat muzak was an apt prelude to Nicol's next post – under the baton of light orchestra conductor Cyril Stapleton. Jimmy was also hired for a session with Cleo Laine, Johnny Dankworth's singing wife, who was as much a *grande dame* of jazz as presenter Noele Gordon was as host of ITV's *Lunch Box*, lightest of light entertainments, in whose studio band a certain Pete York drummed for the money he could not yet earn in various Midlands jazz outfits.

Dick Heckstall-Smith's argument for quitting Johnny Burch for Blues Incorporated, however, had little to do with financial gain: 'I was getting fed up with the pale imitation and copying that went on in the British be-bop scene. For me, it just wasn't exciting – too timorous, too polite. I was happy to play in a blues band because there was much more to do. I felt that much greater use of the saxophone could be made rather than in the limited and repressed way in which they were being used in American blues bands.'[6]

When Dick arrived in the functions room of Soho's Roundhouse pub for Charlie Watts' first rehearsal with Blues Incorporated in January 1962, the newcomer's kit had been assembled already and a jam session was under way with pianist Keith Scott and, on double bass, a teacher called Andy Hoogenboom – who'd brought along a spectator, 21-year-old Shirley Ann Shepherd, then in her final year at Hornsey School of Art. Svelte and with cheekbones to die for, she looked a bit like a blonde edition of Juliette Greco, the thinking man's French actress and spectral high priestess of popular existentialism.

Shirley's humorous and intelligent eyes would sometimes catch Charlie at his drums half-looking at her, half turning away, until the spell was broken when, 'An hour later, the door burst open, and closed again with a huge slam,' recollected Heckstall-Smith. 'It was Cyril carrying a bulging old briefcase. He doesn't even say hello or anything, just grunts. Whilst wildly wrestling with the buckle of his briefcase, he roundly curses, and up-ends the contents – a liquid mass of harmonicas – out on the piano. He was angry that there was a saxophone player in the room. I didn't care, and neither did Alexis. It was Alexis's band, and Cyril had to put up with it. As it turned out, Cyril and I got on very well after he grudgingly admitted that even though I played the saxophone, I could play the blues well.'[6]

While Charlie was taken aback that Davies was leery of jazz – from which Dick's saxophone was inseparable – his rapport, and fascination, with the more bohemian Korner was such that he became a frequent visitor to the Bayswater flat where Alexis lived with his wife, Bobbie, and children who were more steeped in the detours of culture than most, what with hanging prints of Cézanne, Matisse and Chagall, first editions on the bookshelves, and lodgers such as Bill Colyer – Ken's percussionist brother – and Charles Fox, a *Melody Maker* jazz columnist. Of more import to Charlie Watts was that 'the walls were full of records. The hip thing was to have them on the floor as well. All the records had been sent in by record companies, and I thought it was the hippest thing in the world. The whole Alexis set-up was very glamorous to me, something I wanted to be a part of, whether it was musicians, painters or whatever.'[5]

Thanks to the Korners, too, Watts drank in the blues, a form that until then had meant just titles for jazz tracks like 'West End Blues' by Louis Armstrong, and the underlying thrust of, say, 'Chips Boogie Woogie' by Woody Herman or Parker's 'Now's The Time'. When blues was mentioned in *Melody Maker*'s jazz pages, the usual frame of reference was Hoagy Carmichael (eg 'Hong Kong Blues'), the swing-derived sophistications of Big Joe Turner, Jimmy Witherspoon and, further back, Billie Holiday, Fats Waller, Bessie Smith and all that.

Yet blues of a more gutbucket nature had been more than a trace element in British jazz from as long ago as the Crane River ensemble when 'with Ken, Bill, Chris and I being into Leadbelly,' said Lonnie Donegan, 'we featured this with the band.' A strong motivation for Alexis Korner to join Chris Barber's then amateur combo in 1950 had been the acquisition of discs by Leadbelly, Robert Johnson, Big Bill Broonzy and further Mississippi delta legends through Barber's next-door neighbour's relatives in New York.

You'd have had some search then for anything wilder on the BBC Light Programme than *Ken Sekora's Jazz Club*, Friday evening's *Radio Rhythm Club* and infrequent spins of Waller, Carmichael and the odd blues opus between the unchained melodies, Mantovanis, Mambo Italianos and doggies in the window on *Two-Way Family Favourites*. 'I first heard blues on *Radio Rhythm Club*,' recalled Lonnie Donegan, 'but there was very little on wax – or shellac as it was then. Nevertheless, in 1947, I fell in love with Josh White's "House Of The Rising Sun" backed by "Strange Fruit" on black-label Brunswick. After that, I really got into jazz – and there were a lot of jazz records available with blues titles and the likes of Bessie Smith singing blues within the jazz bands.'

Interviewed for the *New Musical Express* in 1955, Humphrey Lyttelton was effusive in his praise for Muddy Waters, one prong of a triumvirate – with Howlin' Wolf and Elmore James – that ruled the blues scene in Chicago. Yet Lyttelton was neither the first nor the most committed blues champion within Britain's jazz community. While he, Ken Colyer and others may have arranged a few bookings for blues artists, it was Chris Barber who sank actual cash into the conservation of the form after overseeing a Big Bill Broonzy concert in 1951. Defying the likelihood of monetary loss, Chris also brought over Sister Rosetta Tharpe in 1957, Sonny Terry and Brownie McGhee in May 1958 and Muddy Waters in December.

Despite past disagreements with Alexis Korner, Barber was also amenable to Blues Incorporated, fresh from rehearsing at the Roundhouse, filling the unbilled interval spot for his Jazz Band that same 1962 month at the Marquee, then in a basement below a cinema in Oxford Street, and the National Jazz Federation's main London venue. Other support spots followed as a result of 'loving self-destruction on his part,' deduced Korner, 'because Chris must have realised that a major R&B boom would kill the trad boom, but he still did it. Chris was the only person who liked us playing electric guitar, but there was only a limited amount of work with him, possibly on Thursday or Wednesday at the Marquee, maybe once a month.

'Then Blues Incorporated played its first couple of concerts as a band, supporting Acker Bilk. The second was at the Civic

Centre in Croydon. It was a riot. Acker did a set, and then we went on and did one, and then Acker came back on. The Bilk fans loathed us to destruction because we were the first loud – by the standards of the day – electric blues band. The Acker concert attracted a certain amount of press, but not much. The odd folk or jazz club which had given us gigs immediately withdrew their patronage as soon as we appeared with amplifiers, so we had to get a club of our own together in another way.'[1]

Along the way, there was to be structural tampering, exemplified by the replacement of Keith Scott with Graham Bond, and Charlie's new friend Andy Hoogenboom with Johnny Dankworth's bass player Spike Heatley, and then the more suitable Jack Bruce. 'It sounded like rock 'n' roll to me,' Bruce confessed, 'but working with Alexis was the most formative, important time of my life.'[4]

It was an education, too, for Charlie, who discovered that just as Earl Palmer served Little Richard, so Earl Phillips, a skilled be-bop drummer, did Jimmy Reed, one of the younger giants of urban blues. 'He'd got such a quirky way of playing,' said Watts of Phillips, 'and Chicago shuffles are technically very difficult to do. They come down on the backbeat so loud, and get this shuffle-like thing in between – it's fantastic – without the feet going. Usually very quiet they play, the old guys – so to me, it was not really any different to jazz to be honest.'[6]

Into the bargain, Blues Incorporated was primarily an instrumental unit reliant on much improvisation after Alexis Korner had found a home for the group in a downstairs room between a jeweller's and the ABC teashop along Ealing Broadway. The new G Club – the blues and nothing but – was patronised straightaway by enthusiasts and curiosity-seekers from other West London suburbs and beyond. While Charlie, Jack, Dick, Alexis, Cyril and featured singer Long John Baldry were semi-permanent fixtures in the turnover of personnel, a constant flux of other players was drawn from an audience embracing individuals for whom record sessions had evolved into endeavours to reproduce the US sounds on guitars and self-conscious voices, some yet to break.

Others preferred to merge into the shadows after descending the steps of a club swiftly nicknamed 'the Moist Hoist' for the dripping condensation that had necessitated the hauling of a tarpaulin over the stage to render overloaded amplifiers with naked wires less lethal and less likely to fall silent midway through a number. Outside, however, passers-by were brought up short by the underpinning four-in-a-bar rhythm. 'What struck me was the beat of the drums,' confirmed Keith Richards, a fan from faraway Kent. 'Before you saw the band, you heard it.'[4]

At Sidcup College of Art, Keith had found that other graphics students shared his interest in the rock 'n' roll end of blues. From messing about on guitars in common room, toilets (for echo) and empty painting studios had evolved not so much a group as a musical appreciation society. The mainstays over a two-year privatised regime were Keith and another guitarist, Dick Taylor. The vocalist was a chap Dick knew from grammar school called Mick Jagger, who had to screw himself up with a couple of beers to snarl a Chuck Berry ditty – very much a borderline case as a blues – with Blues Incorporated one G Club night.

He'd been taken on as Long John Baldry's understudy, but had kept his options open as Keith and Dick wanted to form a group that remained more eagerly abreast of the latest genre developments than former 'trad dad' Alexis and baggy-trousered Cyril, glowering over his harmonica at Heckstall-Smith's too-jazzy sax and Graham Bond's aberrant electric organ. Jagger had strung along when Taylor and Richards were among auditionees for a blues outfit under the aegis of a multi-instrumentalist from Gloucestershire named Brian Jones.

After much umming-and-ahhing from Jones, the unit had boiled down to himself, Richards, Taylor – persuaded to transfer to bass – Jagger and Ian Stewart, an incorrigible boogie-woogie pianist, who worked in Imperial Chemical Industries offices, a stone's throw from Buckingham Palace. Among a moving feast of drummers was former Royal Fusilier Carlo Little of Lord Sutch's Savages – for whom he was also what might be described as 'musical director' in that, as Tony Dangerfield, a later bass guitarist, would recall, 'He drilled me through the act. He'd been in the army, and was like a sergeant-major.'

While Brian was keen on retaining the exacting Carlo, painter and decorator Mick Avory was tolerated for two rehearsals in the light of, purportedly, a near-total ignorance then of even Chuck Berry, let alone Muddy Waters, Howlin' Wolf, Jimmy Reed *et al*. The following year, Avory would respond to a *Melody Maker* 'wanted' advertisement from a 'smart go-ahead group' – which turned out to be The Kinks, a bunch from Muswell Hill, home too of Shirley Ann Shepherd. She was known to Jones, Jagger and the others as the girlfriend of Charlie Watts after a shy courtship began at that Roundhouse rehearsal.

He was out of Jones, Stewart and the Kentish contingent's league professionally, what with Blues Incorporated's first LP yet to be recorded, but scheduled for release in November 1962 (admittedly on Decca's budget subsidiary, Ace of Clubs), yet Charlie would have been the perfect drummer for the group that Brian had just christened The Rolling Stones.

# 4 Stones

'Just a few months earlier, I wouldn't have given their offer a second thought because I was all for modern jazz – but I suppose I had a theory that R&B was going to be a big part of the scene, and I wanted to be in on it.'

*– Charlie Watts*[1]

Though each would stay in the picture by circuitous enquiry about the other's activities, Shirley and Charlie drifted apart after she began a sculpture course at the Royal College in September 1962.

Higher education figured too in conflicting pressures within a still amorphous Rolling Stones, yet to find a regular drummer, and with Dick Taylor torn between accepting a scholarship at the Central School of Art, and continuing in an outfit that, in mid-1962, seemed likely to go nowhere.

In the pantheon of Blues Incorporated splinter groups, the Stones weren't even also-rans, let alone pop-stars-in-waiting. Yet the very idea of becoming one wasn't so much as an afterthought for such as moustachioed, pipe-smoking Graham Bond – who was contemplating whether to sound out Jack Bruce about forming a breakaway unit – or Cyril Davies who, as Alexis Korner alone did at the G Club now, ruled a venue in Harrow-on-the-Hill, fronting his new All-Stars, bereft of the hated saxophone and organ – and with musicians from Lord Sutch's Savages and West Drayton's Cliff Bennett And The Rebel Rousers, among them 16-year-old *wunderkind* Nicky Hopkins on piano, and Carlo Little on drums before his overwhelming Sutch duties necessitated the recruitment of one Bill Eyden.

Despite the rapid turnover of personnel, Blues Incorporated continued to go from strength to strength. Most recently, they'd snared a weekly residency at the Flamingo – though it was the well-attended Thursday nights at the Marquee since May 1962 that had inspired the title of the long-awaited debut album. Nevertheless, *R&B From The Marquee* had been realised in the studio under the supervision of Jack Good, cited by many as the true originator of British pop for being the brains behind *Oh Boy!*, *Cool For Cats* and further television series directed at teenagers via a parade of acts following each other so quickly that the screaming audience, urged on by Good, scarcely had pause to draw breath.

One of Good's final productions before seeking his fortune in the USA, *R&B From The Marquee*, did not feature Charlie Watts, but Graham Burbidge, a Chris Barber Jazz Bandsman. Not only had he taken the trouble to buttonhole a visiting Muddy Waters' drummer, Francis Clay, for a few pointers, but, with a pound sign over every crotchet in Decca's West Hampstead studios, 'Alexis asked me to do it,' said Burbidge, 'because, in his exact words, he didn't think Charlie was up to it.'[2]

Though disappointed, Watts too thought that Graham was more equal than he to this ultimate litmus test of musical competence, particularly at such an important point in Blues Incorporated's career. Just as attractively in his selfless and matter-of-fact candour, he also suggested that, for future stage performances, they might be better off with Ginger Baker, still with The Johnny Burch Octet. In any case, implied Charlie, a double life as a Charles Hobson and Gray employee and Blues Incorporated drummer was burning the candle to the middle.

'During the course of the summer, the band was working more and more,' confirmed Alexis Korner, 'and Charlie had decided that he didn't want to be a professional musician because it was too uncertain an existence.'[3] Charlie was, none the less, pleased to fulfil dates until Baker was able to take over. He also accompanied Korner and the others to Johnny Burch Octet engagements where 'you could hear the thing that Jack and Ginger had between them – and I didn't want to get in the way of that'.[2]

As Baker extricated himself from Burch, Watts pledged himself to the less demanding Blues By Six containing other Blues Incorporated members, past, present and future, Andy Hoogenboom, Keith Scott and saxophonist Art Themen – a junior doctor in a London hospital,[4] who was to replace Graham Bond – as well as, on guitars, former sailor Geoff Bradford (who also sang and wailed harmonica) and, one of Cyril Davies's panel-beating colleagues, Brian Knight. Charlie, Themen and his successor, Dave Gelly, liked talking jazz, but were happy enough tackling a wide spectrum of blues forms from the 1930s rural exorcisms of Scrapper Blackwell to Bo Diddley, who, like Chicago friend and rival Chuck Berry, had managed a crossover from the US 'sepia' chart to its pop Top 20.

Blues By Six's jazzers felt quite fulfilled with a workload that embraced Friday evenings as well as a late afternoon session every Sunday off Leicester Square at Studio 51, England's oldest jazz venue – and less often at the Piccadilly Jazz Club, the Six Bells in Chelsea and intermissions on Thursdays at the Marquee.[5] As these bookings were within comparatively easy reach, Blues By Six relied on buses and either Brian Knight's father's Ford Anglia or Mr Watts's Humber – while the transport of Charlie's kit was eased by leaving it when convenient at the left-luggage office in Leicester Square underground station.

With Blues Incorporated engagements ebbing away, Watts was also freer to drum non-committally with other groups – including The Rolling Stones, sometimes as far afield as Epsom School of Art and the Boy Blue Club in Woking's Atlanta Ballroom, whenever Carlo Little – who'd scribbled Charlie's telephone number on an empty cigarette packet for Brian Jones – or either of their latest needs-must drummers, Steve Harris and Tony Chapman (a travelling salesman), couldn't make it.

The Stones' prospects appeared rosier after a promising if low-profile debut at the Marquee in July, the evening that Blues Incorporated were to perform – with Ginger Baker and 'very suspect tuning and internal balance'[6] – on the Light Programme's *Jazz Club*. Though Mick Avory's name was prominent in what little publicity preceded it, Dick Taylor is certain that Watts was a temporary Stone on that night-of-nights 'because, for reasons best known to himself, Alexis didn't want to use Charlie on the radio, which is bloody stupid because he was really good.

'At the time too, we were getting very fed up with Tony Chapman not turning up. He couldn't keep time either. I remember us making this little cartoon – I think it was Brian Jones's drawing – me with my beard, Brian and his big guitar, Keith with his little dotty eyes, Mick another stick figure and an arrow pointing off the page to Tony Chapman who was in Liverpool at the time he should have been at a rehearsal.

'Charlie came along to quite a few of them, and I noticed that the same chemistry wasn't there when Charlie was with Alexis as when he was with the Stones.'

This was so most of the time. A glaring exception was when the Stones shared a bill in a Harrow church hall with what was now The Graham Bond Trio – with Jack Bruce and Ginger Baker. In order to speed up the equipment changeover between acts, Watts agreed to use Baker's home-made kit of perspex plus *bona fide* African drums of thick, shaved animal skins, 'but I couldn't play it. Nothing would happen. I broke three pairs of sticks. He had them set up so that the angle was all wrong for me.'[7]

As this incident – along with the Graham Burbidge business and the subsequent gradual parting from Blues Incorporated – had not diminished Charlie in their eyes, so he recognised that the

Stones were not marking time like Blues By Six – or Alexis and Cyril, living evidence that you could have the most extensive R&B repertoire in the world, sing like a half-caste nightingale or make a guitar talk, but if you suffered from middle age, obesity or baldness, you'd never get more than a cult following. Whatever your popularity, booking fees would remain at best static because, then as now, most promoters took no account of inflation.

Not that this bothered The Rolling Stones, who could offer both R&B credibility and teen appeal, with Mick Jagger's grotesque beauty and Brian Jones' Beatle-esque blond moptop. Moreover, though Charlie was aware that 'they were working a lot of dates without getting paid or even worrying about it',[8] cash flow was such that Bill Wyman, the bass player enlisted after Dick Taylor decided in favour of the Central School of Art, was able to think seriously of packing in his day job as a storekeeper.

All Charlie had to do was ask and this would be his too. The Stones lacked only the recording deal that would either turn them into more of a commercial proposition or nullify them if the slicker exactitudes of the studio sterilised their *au naturel* impact. Still Watts waited and pondered. One night, he telephoned Bobbie Korner for an unbiased opinion. 'She asked Charlie if he liked the Stones, and he said yes,' remembered her husband. 'She asked if he liked Blues By Six, and he said yes. So she said, "Which group has the most work?" He said the Stones, so she said, "Well, I advise you to join the Stones then, if you like them equally."'[3]

Were the Stones too rock 'n' roll? Brian Knight and Geoff Bradford thought so, but Charlie didn't dislike it on principle as they did, despite outlines dissolving between the Stones and the lurid theatrics of Screaming Lord Sutch via, say, the incorporations of The Coasters' 'I'm A Hog For You Baby' and any number of Chuck Berry items into their respective repertoires. It had, Watts supposed, a shadowy link to jazz, but was controlled by a more stilted discipline. 'Rock 'n' roll is restricting,' he surmised, not disparagingly. 'Jazz breathes – or improvised music breathes. It's got an elasticity to it – which is very hard to do well. There's different volumes you play. Most rock 'n' roll is totally on top. It's just volume the whole time. There's no budging. If you budge, it's wrong. It doesn't work.'[9]

As poker-faced playing rock 'n' roll as he did jazz or blues, Watts looked neither as if he wanted to crawl away and hide – or condescendingly superior, smirking at his jazz cronies at the back, demonstrating to all the world his contempt for this simplistic drivel, as a bass guitarist who shall be nameless had by pumping Buddy Holly's 'Peggy Sue' with one hand in his pocket, an attitude intolerable to The Zombies, who were glad to see the back of him. They held the Market Hall in St Albans as The Beatles did the Cavern, The Animals Newcastle's Club-A-Go-Go – and now the Stones the Craw Daddy at the back of a pub in Richmond, equidistant on the exact opposite side of the Thames to the G Club.

In the offices and factories of Britain today, how many are the fifty- and sixty-somethings who took the then wise course of abandoning 1960s pop groups later to Hit The Big Time? In some parallel dimension, perhaps it's Charlie Watts, not Carlo Little, who turned his back on the Stones to spend years criss-crossing Europe in draughty, overloaded vans with David Sutch, the most famous British pop star who never had a hit. After all, as Charlie would tell you himself, 'I was a bit used to rock 'n' roll. I knew most of the rock 'n' roll guys, people like Screaming Lord Sutch and Nicky Hopkins. I was quite used to Chuck Berry and that.'[10]

Instead, he continued to react instinctively to Blues By Six's 12-bar set-works as some stretches at Studio 51 went by as complete blurs – while circling round the Stones, fascinated by both their angle on R&B and their personalities, especially that of Keith Richards, 'the classic naughty boy. He's the sort of guy I knew at school who hated the head boy.'[11] A healthy balance of differences and commonality between them consolidated the friendship of C-stream Keith, slouching last into class, and Charlie, not exactly form captain material, but a capable if often uninvolved pupil.

For all his loutish affectations, Mick Jagger, then pursuing a degree at the London School of Economics, was half a class higher than Watts and Richards – and, so it transpired, Wyman when they got to know him. Brian Jones was even more genteel, but Charlie was content to be a passive listener as Mick or Brian, arm-wavingly angry or cynically amused by everything, held forth in public bars, rehearsal rooms, parties and during wanderings round central London such as a visit to Drum City in Shaftesbury Avenue where dealer Gerry Evans was to recount selling Watts a second-hand Ludwig – a continental make – on hire purchase 'because he didn't have any money. It was a blue oyster Super Classic, and he loved it. So far as I know, he's still got it. Charlie used to bring this Mick Jagger to the shop with him, and all he was interested in was our maracas.'[12]

Such emporiums were to buy back saleable instruments taking up cupboard space, and monolithic speakers serving as room dividers for ex-members of the groups that had once been as much the embodiment of the British beat boom as more illustrious brethren. It seems so far away now, an aeon almost as bygone as that bracketed by Hitler's suicide and 'Rock Around The Clock', but pop was this sceptr'd isle's chief contribution to world culture during the swinging '60s, one of the most turbulent decades of the last century.

Just as some English history primers start with the Battle of Hastings, the year that divided the Dark Ages from the medieval period of UK pop was 1963, when Liverpool – where nothing used to happen apart from dock strikes – became the most romantic corner of the kingdom with the coming of Merseybeat, spearheaded by The Beatles. After an all-Liverpool edition of ITV's *Thank Your Lucky Stars*, commercial expediency sent all but the dimmest London talent scout up to the Holy City to plunder the musical gold. Accordingly, having been gutted of all its major talents, Liverpool was left to rot as, like pillaging Vikings of old, the contract-waving host next alighted on Manchester where there were also guitar groups that had mastered 'Twist And Shout', 'Fortune Teller', 'Money' and other numbers that became British beat standards.

When it was decided that the Manchester scene had 'finished', the London invaders fanned out to other regions now that every one of them had been deemed to have a 'sound' or a 'beat' peculiar to itself – though somehow a lot of the groups everywhere looked and sounded just like The Beatles.

By the middle of 1963, there came a sign that the search was rebounding conveniently to the capital when Dagenham's Brian Poole And The Tremeloes' version of 'Twist And Shout' penetrated the Top Five. More to the point in the context of this discussion, The Cyril Davies All-Stars, of all people, had been signed to Pye, who'd issued a single, 'Country Line Special', in May – and the *Richmond And Twickenham Times* had, on 13 April 1963, made passing reference to the Stones – and, more incidentally, described Charlie as a 'designer' – when devoting a page to an evening at the Craw Daddy.

It had been three months then since Watts had become an official Rolling Stone – on 14 January at the Flamingo – and a drumming train driver named Derek Manfredi had joined Blues By Six. 'Lots of my friends thought I'd gone raving mad,' grinned Charlie. 'There was me, earning a comfortable living, which obviously was going to nosedive if I got involved with The Rolling Stones.'[8]

He went the whole hog by giving notice at Charles Hobson and Gray – though his boats were only half-burned as the firm implied that, as it was with National Service, his old job might be waiting for him when he got back. He also made ends meet as a freelance commercial artist while roughing it for a while in

Jagger, Jones and Richards' dingy rented flat in Chelsea where 'I'd get up in the morning, and Brian and Keith would be snoring away, and I'd think, "I'm not going to an interview today. We're playing tonight anyway." Suddenly, I was in this band where everybody was clapping. Alexis was a big band to be in, but the Stones had such a mad following, and it got bigger every week. Then The Beatles happened, and it became the thing to be in a beat group.'[13]

# 5  Beat

'When we got Charlie, that really made it for us.'
*– Keith Richards*[1]

For Charlie, there was always the safety net of Mum's home cooking and clean sheets if he needed to get his nerve back for another round of smeared coffee cups, overflowing makeshift ashtrays and pooling loose change for a trip up the off-licence to see him and the other tenants through record-playing sessions and other indoor pursuits that turned afternoon into gone midnight.

'It was actually sitting up endlessly with Keith and Brian,' he remembered. 'I was out of work at the time, and I just used to hang about with them, waiting for jobs to come up, daytime work, just listening to Little Walter and all that, that it got ground in. I learned the blues through Cyril Davies and Alexis Korner. Keith and Brian taught me Jimmy Reed. They also taught me to enjoy Elvis Presley through D.J. Fontana, who I think is a wonderful player. Before that, there was only one record I liked by Elvis.'[2]

When it made abrupt sense to look homeward again – which was soon to be on a different Kingsbury housing estate – Charlie, like Ian Stewart and Bill Wyman, a married father, became more peripheral to the Stones socially. 'He was very much a man of few words,' observed Pat Andrews, one of Brian Jones' girlfriends. 'Just getting on with what he was supposed to do and then going back to his parents' house.'

Nevertheless, Watts and Wyman could now provide a sturdy and fully interlocking rhythmic skeleton which the others were able to veil in musical flesh. Charlie also made a valuable off-stage contribution to the group by designing most of the rather prosaic posters and flyers whenever they were either on a percentage or hiring a venue themselves.

When the Stones were no longer a booker's risk, mere word of mouth would fill the Craw Daddy to overflowing. The rest, as they often say, is history – or would be when, through knowing Brian Epstein, The Beatles' manager, Georgio Gomelsky, the club's promoter, a power in the National Jazz Federation – and the Stones' would-be Epstein – invited The Beatles to look in after they'd recorded a *Thank Your Lucky Stars* at ITV's nearby Teddington studios.

Noting that the Stones were exciting their Craw Daddy audiences as much as his outfit were theirs at the Cavern, lead guitarist George Harrison was to recommend them to soul-tortured Decca recording manager Dick Rowe, who had let The Beatles slip from his then unconcerned clutches early in 1962. Their spectacular rise to national stardom had provoked Rowe to saturate the company with beat groups in hopes that one of them might catch on like its failed Scouse supplicants had to teeth-gnashing effect when seized by Decca's main commercial enemy, EMI.

A more tidy-minded (or lazy) author might represent the Stones' consequent climb to fame like that clichéd movie sequence of dates being ripped off a calendar to a background of clips...a minor chart entry with the first single...into the Top 20 with the next...rows of screaming girls...David Jacobs pressing the 'ding!' button on *Juke Box Jury* for the third 45...a Top Ten placing...the limousine gliding to the sold-out theatre...Number One...wild scenes on the boards and off...police cordons...*The Ed Sullivan Show*...the Hollywood Bowl...and a slow dazzle prefacing the heroes' return to *Sunday Night At The London Palladium*!

Success wasn't quite as instant as that. Instead, like old millstones, the next chapter in the story of the Stones quivered, stirred and groaned reluctantly into its first Tippex-drenched sentence with an off-peak recording session on basic single-track at IBC, one of the most modern and well-equipped studios in central London, arranged via engineer Glyn Johns, who sang with The Presidents, a combo that enjoyed parochial renown in Sutton, the south London suburb where they'd supported the Stones in a local pub. 'I was thrilled,' exclaimed Charlie. 'Glyn Johns did it when they stopped work at 5.30. We did eight tracks in about ten minutes [*sic*], and went off and played at a club.'[3]

The understanding was that IBC was to tape the group for a paper loss in exchange for the rights to exploit the results. This was to be hastily amended to a lump sum after the Stones signed with a two-man management team with more contacts in the industry than Giorgio Gomelsky – who hadn't bound the group to a written contract – and a willingness to sink hard cash into removing them from the treadmill of the clubs.

Eric Easton and Andrew Loog Oldham were an odd couple. Besuited, middle-aged and receding, the former behaved like a stereotypical pop group manager from a monochrome Ealing film like 1959's *Idle On Parade* with Anthony Newley as a conscripted rock 'n' roller. Like Sid James, Newley's on-screen man-of-affairs, Easton seemed as if all he liked about his pop clients was the money they could amass, selling them like tins of beans – with no money back if they tasted funny.

Eric stood pensively at his office window, sun-blanked spectacles flashing over Piccadilly. With his feet on the desk and yapping into the telephone was Andrew, his teenage sidekick. Once he'd aspired to pop stardom himself, but now Andrew saw himself behind the spotlight as a hybrid of a more far-sighted Larry Parnes – the fast-talking 1950s pop Svengali and inspired generator of correlated publicity – and an English 'answer' to Phil Spector, a weedy young New Yorker, who was hot property in the

States for his spatial 'wall of sound' technique, whereby he'd multi-track an apocalyptic *mélange* – replete with everything including the proverbial kitchen sink – behind acts who'd submitted to his master plan. Thus, a potent combination of vocational boredom, lost business innocence and frustrated artistic aspirations had taken Andrew Oldham to the suffocating crush of the Craw Daddy and a desire to steer the Stones out of it.

Before it ended in tears, there was enough common ground between bombastic *parvenu* Oldham, lost in wonder at the Stones, and Easton, the hard-nosed traditionalist for whom wads of notes were preferable to the acclaim of the Great British Public, for each to be prone to both thrift and extravagance when presenting The Rolling Stones to the nation.

The attitude at Decca, however, was not to waste too many resources on this new breed of pop group: all of them are the same, and none of them will last long anyway. Yet, fully aware of the buzz emanating from Richmond, Dick Rowe was ready, despite finding Andrew Loog Oldham personally objectionable, to make hay while the sun shone for his and Eric Easton's discovery before this beat bubble burst and 'decent' music could reign once more.

Though it was alien to Decca's policy, Rowe let Oldham attempt to produce the Stones' maiden A-side, 'Come On', in Olympic, an independent studio in Barnes. However, it was to be remade at the firm's West Hampstead complex during regulated Musicians' Union hours – and with regulated musicians at the end of a telephone should the lads' lean recording experience show too much. Of all instrumentalists, drummers were most likely to be ghosted by someone more technically accomplished, because beat groups were inclined to accelerate and slow down *en bloc* to inconsistencies of tempo caused by the mood of the hour. In the early 1960s, among those earning their tea breaks in this fashion were ex-Kenny Ball Jazzman Ron Bowden, Jimmy Nicol, Clem Cattini of The Tornados and The Vic Lewis Orchestra's Andy

White, who – with no slight on Ringo Starr intended – had been heard on The Beatles' maiden single, 'Love Me Do'.

The Stones, however, were all present and correct on 'Come On'. If he was bothered by the memory of *R&B From The Marquee* and Graham Burbidge, Charlie Watts proved as competent on disc as on the boards, though he found that, 'I hate playing with cans [earphones] on. I always play with one on and one off.'[4] Besides, any injury to his pride by the arrival of a substitute would have been academic anyway as the Olympic version was chosen for release on 7 June 1963, with 'I Want To Be Loved', one of the IBC tracks, as its B-side.

Charlie was a less irregular surveyor of the hit parade these days, and was elated when 'Come On' reached a tantalising high of Number 20 in the *New Musical Express* list. Sales had been spurred on by a televisual debut on *Thank Your Lucky Stars* after the ticklish operation of retaining the services of Ian Stewart, whose piano section had been rendered inaudible on the instructions of Oldham, who felt that the burly ex-ICI pen-pusher with his slicked-back haircut lacked visual appeal. There was no denying, Oldham explained, that he was a bit, well...you know.

Stewart wasn't, therefore, required to squeeze into the uniform stage costumes that Andrew and Eric had procured for the fellows to wear on television. He could carry on as an official member of the group as long as he remained out of sight. He was disgusted that no one made much more than a perfunctory attempt to disagree. Nevertheless, an understandable dark night of the ego passed, and Stewart stayed on as general factotum, whose duties included humping equipment and, like an army batman without the uniform, attending to the others' food, sleep and general health requirements.

With the M1 only half-completed, Ian also had to cope with the tactical problems of moving the operation from A to B so that the Stones were on time for a ten-minute spot twice nightly during the first half of an all-styles-served-here autumn package tour with, initially, two North American acts as the principal draws. This would interrupt a long run of one-nighters on the ballroom circuit, doing battle against adverse acoustics – and adverse audiences. Having little in the way of seating on purpose, dancing was encouraged, and hall managers expected groups to exude a happy, inoffensive on-stage atmosphere as well as action-packed sound to defuse potential unrest among over-excited adolescents. Fists often swung harder than the musicians, who maintained ghastly grins as they soundtracked someone being half-killed out there.

In venues where the personality of the band was generally secondary to brawling and the pursuit of romance, the Stones were immediately conspicuous for their motley appearance in days when it was incumbent upon beat groups to have an almost Midwich Cuckoo regularity of dress and hairstyle. It had been Charlie who'd led the rebellion by 'losing' his *Thank Your Lucky Stars* check jacket. There was also a general tendency within the group to sport hair that, if not up to Lord Sutch's shoulder-length standards yet, was enough to brand them 'queers' in country towns where the Second World War was about to enter its 25th year.

Within a minute of the show's start, a roughneck might have to be restrained physically by Ian Stewart from slamming his fist through a public address speaker, having decided to be a lion of justice, striking a blow for decent entertainment for decent folk. Yet such attention was not typical. Most onlookers would keep their distance, and the set might end with long seconds of thunderstruck hush until a spatter of clapping crescendoed into a whistling, cheering, stamping tumult.

Some caught the group a second and even third time during this round of engagements, and there'd be a noticeable rippling stagewards a few dramatic bars into the opening number. These new fans might have simply jived to the other worthy but less rough-and-ready acts on offer such as The Hollies – touted as

'Manchester's Beatles' – with ex-Fentone Bobby Elliott rattling the traps. To the untrained ear, he was just thumping out a backbeat that a half-wit couldn't lose, but Charlie could tell that Bobby's heart was in jazz too, and that he was 'a really good player'[3] from subtleties like a latent trademark roll that dated back to Art Blakey.

On the round-Britain tour that followed, Watts also watched The Everly Brothers – or, to be precise, the duo's 'fabulous drummer, Jim Gordon. We'd never seen a band as slick as that.'[3] From the wings, too, both Charlie and Mick were captivated by 'incredible'[3] Jerome Green, who wielded the maracas that coalesced the shave-and-a-haircut-six-pence undercurrent to Bo Diddley's eponymous signature tune.[5]

By the final concert at the Hammersmith Odeon on 3 November, no one could pretend that Diddley and The Everly Brothers were the jaunt's *de facto* main attraction any more, even if they wouldn't relinquish their headlining supremacy. The Stones were still a few months short of 'It's All Over Now', their first chart-topper, but they'd been recognised in corner shops and wayside petrol stations, and that mingled antagonism, dull watchfulness and grudging ovation would defer to a different atmosphere altogether when the ballroom dates were resumed. Reading's boss group, The Moquettes, preceded the Stones at a midnight matinée in Tottenham, where vocalist Keith Neville was astounded when 'on our arrival at the stage door, the girls were screaming and getting very excited, thinking that we were the Stones. The queue was right round the centre of Tottenham – so you can imagine the atmosphere inside. It was heaving, just a sea of heads.'[6]

That one-nighters were beset with unprecedented difficulties now was instanced further by Charlie's rage on the occasion – or, perhaps, not such an occasion nowadays – when some of those crammed closest to the front were able to wriggle through an inadequate barrier of stewards. Afterwards, he was almost killed with kindness by libidinous females not much younger than himself, who ripped his new pink shirt so thoroughly that he could never wear it again.

'He suddenly got thrown into the thing that was really not part of his self image,' said Keith Richards.[7] There were, however, off-stage compensations. With the Stones' second 45, 'I Wanna Be Your Man', in the Top 20 and no steady girlfriend since Shirley, Watts had sudden access to plenty of unsteady ones for whom his face on the very first edition of *Top Of The Pops* proved a powerful aphrodisiac. A strong motive for any young man, no matter how high-minded, becoming a pop icon – especially in the Swinging '60s – was that no matter what you looked like, you can still be popular with young ladies. Look at Ringo and his nose. Look at Bernard Dwyer, resembling more a used car salesman than a drummer in Freddie And The Dreamers. Look at Bobby Elliott, far too young to be losing his hair.

Yet, with middle-aged candour, Charlie Watts would insist that, 'I wasn't interested in being a pop idol. It's not the world I come from. It's not what I wanted to be, and I still think it's silly.'[8]

His little period of no-strings frivolity ended after Shirley Ann Shepherd, quite unchanged, re-entered his life after being allowed past backstage security, when the Stones were at the Hammersmith Odeon. With old affections flooding their hearts, the two were to holiday together in Gibraltar the following spring[9] having resolved to marry as soon as the sweep of events permitted.

A third hit, 'Not Fade Away', had heralded the climb of the Stones' first LP to Number 19 in the *singles* chart, signifying that sales of the 45s were but a surface manifestation of the respect accorded the group for their natural vitality and musicianship by sixth-formers, undergraduates and the like who bought albums as their younger siblings did singles. It also triggered the publication of a glossy monthly periodical devoted solely to the Stones; only The Beatles and – for four editions – Gerry And The Pacemakers had also been accorded that accolade.

Like 'Not Fade Away', *The Rolling Stones* had been taped during breaks in the remorseless schedule of driving, driving, driving to strange towns, strange venues and strange beds. Most of the sessions took place at IBC where they transgressed union stipulations by running over into open-ended graveyard hours during which there was room for such experiments as Charlie swathing his drums with an overcoat.

Then it was back to zig-zagging across the country, seeing nothing of Brighton, Glasgow, Plymouth, you name it, apart from what was glimpsed as you strode across the pavement from van to stage door. When asked about what such-and-such a town had been like, Charlie was damned if he could even find it on a map.

# 6 Silence

'I loved the adulation when we were onstage. After that,
I hated it – when you couldn't walk down the road
without people running after you, literally. That was the
most awful period of my life.'

*– Charlie Watts* [1]

British youth culture was now divided into two principal
factions: Mods and, of corresponding uniformity, Rockers, with
their brilliantined ducktails, real or imitation leather jackets,
jeans, motorbike boots, backdated taste in music and hostility
towards interlopers into ordained hang-outs like the Ace Cafe on
London's North Circular Road. If a fixture on its jukebox, a hit
in late 1964 entitled 'Terry' by Twinkle was banned on ITV's
*Ready Steady Go* pop show – for being about a Rocker.

Stones singles didn't sound out of place in the Ace either, but
partly because they conformed to *Ready Steady Go*'s Mod
specifications – 'Caveman types who are Mods at the same time,'
reckoned *Teenbeat Annual* [2] – the group could always count on
the programme, as vital in its way as *Oh Boy!* had been in the
late 1950s, whenever they had a new release to plug.

*Ready Steady Go* belonged more to the Stones than The
Beatles for reasons summarised by 16-year-old David Cook –
later 1970s film actor and pop star David Essex – a habitué of
the Flamingo, which had started advertising itself as 'the
Swinging Club of Swinging London'. He considered that The
Beatles' compromising four-song spot on 1963's *Royal Variety*

*Show* 'meant that they couldn't be any good'.[3] For David, they had 'matured' too quickly and, like Tommy Steele before them, would be soft-shoe shuffling before you could blink. More to Cook's taste were The Rolling Stones, The Kinks, The Pretty Things, Them, The Downliners Sect and other 'hairy monsters' detested by adults.

Almost everywhere nowadays, boys would risk suspension from school for cultivating hair that touched their ears – though one who arrived at his secondary modern one 1964 morning with a Yul Brynner all-off was sent home on the grounds that it was just as attention-seeking, and a prim headmistress in Sydney, Australia, barred not only the wearing of Beatle moptops – by girls as well as boys – but also membership of fan clubs and the carrying of pop star pin-ups in satchels.

Yet Top 20 selections were heard over the sound systems at football stadiums before the match; The Dave Clark Five's early hits being particularly popular for the neo-military percussive hooks that the terraces stamped out on cue.

After his father bought him a Rogers drum kit just like Dave Clark's, David Cook joined R&B outfit The Everons.[4] I gather from my teenage sons that 'R&B' doesn't mean the same now as it did when I was a lad – which, likewise, didn't mean the same as it did when Charlie Watts, ten years older, was a lad. Whereas Charlie absorbed the Mississippi and Chicago vinyl templates, my concept of the stuff for much of my adolescence was derived from Caucasian beat groups of the mid-1960s attempting to emulate the Hookers, Howlin' Wolves and Berries of black America.

The Rolling Stones were the patron saints of all of them: the hopeless, the hopeful and the genuinely talented acts like The Spencer Davis Group, whose Pete York would cite meeting singing guitarist Davis at Birmingham's Excelsior Jazz Club in 1964 as the most fateful juncture of his career, 'though it didn't seem so at the time'. Similar encounters informed the lives of

Keith Hartley and Aynsley Dunbar, successive drummers with Liverpool's Rory Storm And The Hurricanes, who would each garner a greater celebrity with John Mayall's Bluesbreakers and then as leaders of their own blues-based ensembles.

Back in London, Dick Taylor had left the Central School of Art to form The Pretty Things. Three successive drummers – all called Viv – passed through the ranks. The last one, Viv Prince, was the most distinguished, his father being the leader of The Harry Prince Five, omnipresent in the dance halls of pre-war Loughborough. After Harry had taught him the essentials of drumming, Viv had developed a technique that was too quick for the eye to follow when on the boards. This was, nevertheless, moderated on The Pretty Things' first two singles – which seemed to follow the same trajectory as those of the Stones: 'Rosalyn' crept into the Top 30 after they'd mimed to it on *Thank Your Lucky Stars*, while 'Don't Bring Me Down' would be on the edge of the Top Ten four months later. Projected as wilder, fouler and more peculiar than the Stones – sort of Terry-Thomas to their David Niven – the Things stirred up coverage in both the *News Of The World* and the new *Sunday Times* colour supplement.

There are also God-slot TV discussions concerning the depth to which pop had sunk with championship of such reprobates as the Things and the Stones. Indeed, in 1965, three of the latter group – Jagger, Jones and Wyman – were to be fined for relieving themselves against a wall in a petrol station forecourt, despite the defending counsel calling Watts and Richards to testify to their colleagues' good characters.

One of Colchester's Fairies, another bunch of temperamental, long-haired ne'er-do-wells, had caused death by dangerous driving, and a Pretty Things road manager was prosecuted after some unpleasantness with a shotgun following an engagement in Swindon – and, remembers vocalist Phil May, 'in Stockport one night, some screaming bird tore my shirt during the first set, and

Viv Prince stopped drumming to rip her blouse and bra off, and sock her in the mouth'.

Many rungs below the Things and, to a greater degree, the Stones, were the likes of The Cheynes, Gary Farr And The T-Bones – who introduced the tambour to British pop – The Mark Leeman Five, The Roadrunners, The Artwoods, Hereford's Shakedown Sound (who would mutate into Mott The Hoople), Blue Sounds from Leeds, The Peddlers, The Troggs and countless others, some containing stars-in-waiting, but all of them scrimmaging round the more insalubrious beat clubs that were littering British towns. Who couldn't understand envy at the one engagement per week that netted the same as that pocketed by bass guitarist Paul Samwell-Smith for five days as an electrical engineer since his Yardbirds had taken over the Stones' residency at the Craw Daddy in spring 1963, and drummer Jim McCarty dared to tell his mother that he was about to chuck in his soul-destroying job in the City to become a full-time Yardbird?

In a similar position at Sheffield's King Mojo, The Sheffields – like The Mark Leeman Five, The Peddlers and The Artwoods – were exactly 19 years ahead of 1983's brief jazz craze, headed by Carmel and Animal Nightlife. The Sheffields' best-remembered release was an ambitious beat group treatment of vibraphonist Milt Jackson's 'Bag's Groove', which they retitled 'Skat Walking', commensurate with its wordless vocal duet. First recorded by The Miles Davis All-Stars in 1954, this brave updating had no precedent in a pop context. If too clever for the charts, 'Skat Walking' went down a storm in concerts like that held at Birmingham Town Hall on 11 September 1964 when, according to a random survey, The Sheffields stole the show from Blue Sounds, the headlining Blues Incorporated and the Second City's own Spencer Davis Group and Moody Blues.

Straighter pop groups had traced that R&B scent less radically by ditching stage suits and fab-gear winsomeness for longer hair and scruffy taciturnity. The Atlantix of Burton-on-

Trent, for example, played a farewell engagement before reforming the next week as denim-clad Rhythm And Blues Incorporated. Just as prosaic in name and style were The Beaconsfield Rhythm And Blues Group, and, sons of Grantham, The Rhythm And Blues Group. All Hohner Bluesvampers and 'Hoochie Coochie Man' too were Southampton's Howlin' Wolves, The Boll Weevils from dem ole cottonfields of Erdington, Sam Spade's Gravediggers from Coventry and two separate entities called The King Bees (one led by David Bowie).

Nevertheless, too soon for the stronger budgetary commitment to albums beginning in the later 1960s, most R&B groups that wanted to stay in business remained geared for *Top Of The Pops* – and, as 1965 got under way, there was cause for optimism. The *Melody Maker*'s Pop 50 for January showed the Stones in retreat from Number One with an arrangement of Howlin' Wolf's 'Little Red Rooster', colliding with up-and-coming Them and their riveting 'Baby Please Don't Go' from the portfolio of Mississippi rambler Big Joe Williams. Not far ahead was The Animals' Top Tenner, 'Inside Looking Out' – originally recorded as 'My Rebirth'. Wilfully devoid of a whistleable tune to carry its harrowing prison narrative, it had been tried by Eric Burdon during a 1965 jam with Blues Incorporated under the more genteel title of 'Rosie'.

Yet R&B had regressed, sneered Kenny Ball, to 'rock 'n' roll with a mouth-organ',[5] thanks to these superficially exciting groups who'd sucked Chuck Berry and Bo Diddley into its vortex, and were commercialising soul, gospel and every other black musical form going. 'The Group plays poppy R&B,' chirped Spencer Davis, 'and we aim for a good dancing beat.'[6] So did Manfred Mann – once The Mann-Hugg Blues Brothers – after 1963's '5 4 3 2 1' and the comparable Top 20 placing of its 'Hubble Bubble' follow-up enabled them to adjust to the notion of a long-term chart career.

Unlike Manfred Mann, the Stones chose not to span idioms like modern jazz and showbiz evergreens. Nevertheless, while R&B was also their stylistic starting point, they ventured further than Blues Incorporated ever had towards the modern black sounds of North America while making irresistible and danceable concessions to the good, honest trash of hardline pop. However, the Stones' recording of such as Marvin Gaye's 'Can I Get A Witness', The Drifters' 'On The Boardwalk' – complete with 'fool' deep bass second vocal – and the feyer fruits of Jagger and Richards' songwriting partnership ('As Tears Go By', say, or 'The Singer Not The Song') put an end to whatever regard was still felt for them by blues purists and narrow-minded jazzers.

To the common-or-garden teenager in Solihull or Swansea, however, the Stones were not only the brightest stars in the R&B firmament, but an even closer second to The Beatles than Gerry And The Pacemakers, The Searchers and The Dave Clark Five had been. For weeks in 1964, 'It's All Over Now' and 'A Hard Day's Night' had monopolised the first two positions in the British charts (necessitating the avoidance of such revenue-draining clashes in future) until brought down by Manfred Mann's 'Do Wah Diddy Diddy' which in turn fell when 'Have I The Right' by The Honeycombs and The Kinks' 'You Really Got Me' tied at Number One.

The Kinks and The Honeycombs represented the new polarisations of the beat boom. Born of the R&B scene rather than mainstream pop, The Kinks were built to last longest, and they notched up several more early smashes by sticking largely to the same riff-based format and borrowing the Stones' angry scowls and sexual suggestiveness for their stage show. The Honeycombs, on the other hand, were light and instant, with big smiles and a gimmick female drummer.

Yet, however much their aficionados might have refuted the suggestion, The Kinks – and the Stones – were as much part of the UK pop scene as The Honeycombs – and Twinkle, Herman's

Hermits, Cilla Black, Freddie And The Dreamers, Tom Jones, Dusty Springfield, The Beatles and everyone else at the *NME* Pollwinners Concert at Wembley's Empire Pool on 11 April 1965, an afternoon extravaganza that encapsulated the beat boom during its hysterical high summer. Though subsiding to mere cheers for Twinkle, Dusty and Cilla, tidal waves of screams hurled rampaging girls towards crash barriers where they'd be flung back by flushed bouncers, shirt-sleeved in the heat, and aggravatingly nearer to John, Paul, George, Ringo, Herman, Tom, Mick, Brian, Bill, Keith and, yes, Charlie than those who'd sell their souls to be. In the boiling mêlée further back, unluckier ticket-holders burst into tears, rocked foetally, flapped programmes and scarves, tore at their hair, wet themselves and fainted with the thrill of it all.

The lamentable incident with the pink shirt was a mere bagatelle in comparison to later occupational hazards affecting Charlie. Among the gonks, jelly babies, toilet rolls inscribed with messages of undying love and further votive offerings cascading on to the stage one evening in Cardiff, came a pellet from someone's hateful airgun. A travesty of legitimate admiration, it embedded itself in Charlie's face, but, being a man of 'the show must go on' stamp, he kept his cool, hunched lower and carried on playing, wiping away the blood when he could.

Less deplorable had been the Mad Mod Ball, at the Empire Pool once again, where some of the 30 fans arrested had pulled Watts backwards off his stool three times – just as others had similarly at Bristol's Colston Hall, the tom-toms rolling away, left and right.

Unless Authority stopped the show – which Authority often did – Watts was banging out 30 minutes of unheard music night after artless night while weighing up the cash benefits of being a Rolling Stone against his self-picture as a musician. The privacy of the recording studio was pleasant to contemplate from the stage at the Odeon in Rochester or the Bradford Gaumont where transitions from choruses to middle eights were cluttered, and lead guitar breaks wantonly slap-dash.

As well as making his presence felt on Stones record dates, Charlie had also had a hand in autumn 1964's *16 Hip Hits* by the newly created Andrew Oldham Orchestra for Ace of Clubs. While endeavouring to live his Phil Spector dream, Oldham was also emulating Beatles producer George Martin, whose *Off The Beatle Track* LP, with a similar assembly of mostly session musicians, had paid for itself – as would the self-explanatory *Kinky Music* for The Larry Page Orchestra, conducted by the 'You Really Got Me' hitmakers' manager.

On *16 Hip Hits* and later albums by the musicians under Oldham's baton, Rolling Stones items were syndicated – as well as acclamatory originals like 'There Are But Five Rolling Stones' – which might have touched a raw nerve in Ian Stewart, whose piano allied with Charlie's thrashing beat as this instrumental's selling point when it B-sided a certain Cleo's revival of 'To Know Him Is To Love Him' by role model Spector's trio, The Teddy Bears. Then there was '365 Rolling Stones (One For Every Day Of The Year)', a single whose coupling, 'Oh I Do Like To See Me On The B-Side', earned Watts a credit as co-writer as he would as musical director for 'Animal Duds' by Jeannie And The Redheads, Oldham charges who may not have had any physical form beyond the studio.

Charlie's ego was massaged infinitely more by the publication on 17 January 1965 of his 30-page *Ode To A High-Flying Bird*. He'd been coaxed to blow the dust off this largely pictorial hosanna to Charlie Parker after John Lennon, another ex-art student turned pop icon, had led the way the previous March by collating his verse, stories and messy cartoons for *In His Own Write*, the first of two immediate best-sellers for the same imprint, Jonathan Cape.

It was very much a reflection of John's image as the quirkiest Beatle. Charlie's more considered tome was judged to be 'less way-out than Lennon's' in a *New Musical Express* critique,[7] but many interested readers weren't able to so much as browse *Ode To A High-Flying Bird*, let alone buy it. 'The stores wouldn't take it because of what it was'[8] served as an explanation from an author who when asked for a keepsake by a fan, proffered her a chair.

Already, some journalists were wondering if Watts wasn't just as screwy as Lennon on the quiet. During one televised and scream-rent performance, Jagger had waved him to the central microphone to announce 'I Wanna Be Your Man', but Charlie's public articulations were relatively infrequent. He justified this with 'If someone asks me a direct question, I give a direct answer. Anyway, it's becoming a tradition that beat group drummers shouldn't be the greatest talkers.'[9] Only too glad to take a back seat at press conferences, he was typecast as 'the Silent Stone' – just as Ringo Starr was as the Beatle 'who'd play it smoggo. I don't mind talking. It's just that I don't do it very much.'[10]

These remarks by Starr had been echoed curtly by Watts just prior to the Stones' first show at the Olympia in Paris in this nervously brilliant dialogue between himself and a journalist with the clipped solemnity of someone speaking in a language not his own:

'You are called the Silent Stone.'

'Yes'.

'Why is this so?'

'Because I don't talk much.'[11]

In the auditorium, the fans were going as crazy as only fans can go. Yet the damage inflicted within France's premier music hall was but a fraction of the final assessment after the riot spilled into the boulevards where, with hormones raging and armed with bits of broken chair, 2,000 teenagers let off steam in a two-hour orgy of brawling and vandalism in the teeth of tear gas, police dogs and water cannon.

# 7 Marriage

'He's managed to remain serene and calm through all the chaos of the last couple of years.'

*– Brian Jones*[1]

Charlie and Shirley tied the knot on 14 October 1964. They didn't tell what was now the Stones' high command – Oldham, Richards and Jagger – of their intentions until the deed had been done, guessing that the information would be received with acute irritation – notably by Andrew, who, for all his 'new broom' effect upon pop management strategy, had learnt his craft in an age when a pop star would lose fans if he got married. On the other hand, though brokenhearted females had mobbed London's Caxton Hall on that dark day in 1954 when crooner Dickie Valentine and his bride signed the register, he'd survived the decade as a chart contender – and the drummer getting hitched wouldn't affect the Stones' popularity like it would if it had been frontman Mick.

To confound a nosy world, the ceremony had taken place midweek at Bradford Registry Office with a reception miles across the Yorkshire dales in a country pub near Ripon. Among few witnesses were Andy Hoogenboom and his wife, but news leaked out within a fortnight. Though encouraged by Chrissie Shrimpton, Jagger's spirited girlfriend, to do otherwise, Shirley kept a low profile as, initially, Charlie denied that he was no longer a bachelor.

The crisis passed, and any bad blood between the newly-weds and Andrew was diluted. Indeed, Mr and Mrs Watts were to dwell eventually in an apartment with Oldham's London office on the floor above (and that of The Who's management below). When it was necessary to share hotel rooms, it was Charlie and Andrew when it wasn't Charlie and Ian Stewart – or, whenever practical, Charlie and Shirley – though there was some now-forgotten annoyance that caused Watts to look up from watching television, stare into space for a few seconds, rise from his armchair, knock Oldham unconscious, and sit down again.

Overall, however, the Stones had the personal manager they deserved. When press hounds circled the group, whereas Brian Epstein might have cringed if zany merriment about mini-skirts and haircuts swung in seconds to unfunny quips about more inflammable issues, Oldham was all for expletives, gesturing with cigarettes, frankness about drugs and free love, and a general winding-up of adult rage and derision to ensure that the Stones would be as rabidly worshipped by the young. Yet, in cold print, the so-called Silent Stone's ripostes often seemed blandly pedestrian. 'We're great friends with all of them', was Charlie's comment on rivalry with The Beatles.[2] In mitigation, a certain drollness was lost on the page, and a lot of questions he endured were as banal and as repetitious as a stuck record.

Yet, to alleviate the tedium in this bandroom or that chartered flight, there were instances of him being more forthcoming, even garrulous, towards even the most ill-informed, patronising journalist. 'I get bored anywhere,' he explained. 'The only time I'm not bored is when I'm drawing, playing the drums or talking. I talk a lot about nothing usually – and all contradictory. Shirley always accuses me of having no beliefs. Maybe that's why I can talk to anyone.[3]

Now and then, he'd crack back as snappily and as impudently as Mick, Bill, Keith or Brian. What about the future? 'We don't know. It depends on who drops the bomb and when.'[2] Challenged about flicking cigarette ash into a coffee cup, he reasoned, 'Yes, well, it saves stamping them on the floor and making a mess when people don't supply ashtrays.'[4] Watts also proved himself a natural before the cameras in *Charlie Is My Darling*, a documentary shot during a brief trip to Ireland in January 1965, chatting in some backstage alcove about his limitations as a musician without the remotest hint of false modesty.

Having flexed their muscles with the British media, the Stones were fully mobilised by the time they'd been foisted on North America where Britain had hitherto been seen as merely a furbisher of nine-day wonders like Lonnie Donegan, who 'didn't see success over there as long term. The main personal incentive for me going over for that first promotional visit was to see all the jazz musicians I admired live in New Orleans and Birdland in New York, all expenses paid.'

That could almost have been Charlie Watts talking. While he'd recall spending spare moments 'downstairs, going through the jazz collection'[5] during the Stones' two days of sessions at Chess Studios in Chicago where Waters, Wolf, Berry *et al* had recorded their R&B classics, 'New York was *it*. I never really wanted any more. In those days, the only way to get to New York was in a band on a cruise ship. I was lucky to get there before Birdland closed. I saw Charlie Mingus there with a 13-piece band. I also saw a marvellous Sonny Rollins period, where the band would stop, and Sonny would just go on for hours. *That* was America.'[6]

Beyond rapture too would be Krupa with a trio in the Metropole on Broadway, and Earl Hines brushing to Wes Montgomery's soft fretboard swing. Watts seized every opportunity to catch in their natural habitats Gillespie, Roach and other names that had made life worth living at Tyler's Croft. The most pivotal such event was probably hearing Miles Davis's latest incarnation with 19-year-old Tony Williams fusing a rock beat with a busy jazz sensibility. 'He was incredible. A marvellous player, still one of the best actually. I immediately asked Gretsch to send me a kit like his.'[7]

If a long time arriving, a 1957 model would be Charlie's eternal favourite, with its natural maple tom-toms (the smaller one mounted on a snare drum stand), maple-shell snare and bass drum, and four cymbals on Gretsch Techware stands.

From the mid- to late-1960s, Watts would be using some kind of customised Gretsch, but, between 1963 and then, he'd usually be seen behind a Ludwig, the standard group kit for most of the 1960s after Ringo Starr inflicted untold injury on home trade by shelling out for a brown one with Swiss-made Paiste cymbals. Partly because it travelled with The Beatles – and then the Stones – every other stick-wielder from schoolchildren to chart-riding professionals like Chris Curtis of The Searchers and The Fourmost's Dave Lovelady beat a Ludwig too. Nevertheless, Bobby Elliott and Carlo Little shilly-shallied between Ludwig and Britain's own Premier, while Bernard Dwyer stuck with a Trixon kit from Germany – like Ludwig – and, eventually, so would Dave Clark after his Rogers was raffled for charity.

In his regular column in *Midland Beat*, among valuable tips from his own strict practice rota, plus learned critiques of the latest kit accessories, Pete York twitted Clark – as most of the industry's intelligentsia did[8] – while esteeming Keith Moon, now with The Who, as 'the Elvin Jones of the pop world'.[9] A known prankster and exhibitionist, Moon would create havoc from nothing; the most documented example being his disruption of a party in Chertsey by steering a Rolls-Royce Silver Cloud into the host's swimming pool. However, though his antics necessitated extreme sanctions by the group, this was balanced by his principal asset: a wild-eyed performance which, though gratuitously busy, still maintained a precise backbeat. Much of Moon's methodology had been gleaned from Viv Prince, who deputised when Keith was indisposed and, in 1966, recorded a solo single entitled 'Minuet For Ringo'.

This dedication was yet another indication of how famous rather than how skilful a drummer Starr had become. Within professional circles, he was deemed less worthy of respect than lapsed jazzmen like York, Elliott, John Steel of The Animals – and Charlie Watts, 'the only drummer who leaves out more than I do,' said Ringo.[10] The antithesis of Prince and Moon, Watts was becoming outstanding for his stylistic frugality. Like a vicar shy of sermons, he took no solos and favoured only the most essential embellishments beyond a plain beat[11] – such as a recurring rataplan in 'Get Off Of My Cloud' and a floor-tom rumble to bring in the vocal on 1966's '19th Nervous Breakdown'.

As well as taking no unnecessary risks in the studio, Charlie was also less ready than other drummers to unwind during the post-soundcheck jam sessions that sometimes occupied time before a show – and, as for sitting in at the jazz clubs he visited, 'No, it'd scare the life out of me. I'm not very good at that.'[7]

All the same, Watts was acknowledged as a yardstick of excellence for any aspiring pop drummer by such as Clem Cattini, Hal Blaine – who, after serving Phil Spector, was to be heard on as many US hits as Cattini was on British ones – Levon Helm of Bob Dylan's backing Hawks, and Jim Keltner – from an Oklahoman family of percussionists – who was in Gary Lewis And The Playboys, the proudly American exception during that 1965 week when the US Top Ten was otherwise all British.

'Every drummer's main influence in the 1960s was Charlie and Ringo,' opines Alan Barwise. 'They both had incredible grooves that were immediately identifiable. Charlie was the perfect drummer for the Stones in the same way as Ringo was for The Beatles. Could you imagine Buddy Rich or Keith Moon in the Stones? Charlie didn't play loud or was a hard-hitter like the jazzers he admired. It wasn't a driving Buddy Rich approach, just whatever was totally appropriate for a given song. On stage, when Charlie was brilliant, the Stones were brilliant. When the Stones weren't brilliant, Charlie was still brilliant. It was just that the others wouldn't have synched in with him.'

To the less erudite critic in a 1966 edition of *Melody Maker*, 'Paint It Black', the follow-up to '19th Nervous Breakdown', was memorable for 'Charlie's driving tom-tom drumming, a sitar sound and Mick's special Indian lament voice. Charlie creates a galloping beat suggesting high-speed elephants, and Mick's accents get progressively more curried.' [12] In an attempt to make the song exude a more pungent breath of the Orient, Watts would admit ruefully that 'We ruined a marvellous pair of tablas, trying to be Indians. You're not supposed to use sticks on them.' [6]

By 1966, virtually everything the Stones released was a Jagger–Richards opus with the others there to lend power to their patterns of chords and rhymes. 'I try to help them get what they want,' averred Watts, [6] who would extend his percussive skills with bongo-tapping, timpani-pounding and conga-thudding at selected points on *Aftermath*, an LP that ranks with The Kinks' contemporaneous *Face To Face* as an aural abstraction of swinging London.

On the succeeding album, *Between The Buttons*, Charlie was to the fore on the back cover with his sardonic and decidedly non-*High-Flying Bird* stanzas and six-frame cartoon loaded with pokes at the posturing hypocrisy of the music industry – the fake sincerity, the mental sluggishness, the back-stabbing, the cloth-eared ignorance.

Predicting only fleeting prosperity for the beat boom, it was milking the Stones as dry as it could with as little as six weeks between singles, draining them off LPs if need be, in some territories. In North America, the group was like human cargo, shunting from state to state with the drum kit set up on a trolley to facilitate speedier assembly of equipment for a recital that might or might not culminate in a riot. 'We never finished a show for about a year,' sighed Charlie, 'because someone would get hurt in the front row, and we'd have to stop, or it would be chaos and people would run all over the stage. It didn't help my drumming much, but it was just part of being with The Rolling Stones.'[6]

'Charlie took it all with a wry smile,' observed Don Craine of The Downliners Sect, whose activities were confined to the domestic and European markets. In other continents, he also appeared to be *dans sa peau* to comparative strangers. In Australia with the Stones, Frank Allen of The Searchers – who'd just covered 'Take It Or Leave It' from *Aftermath* – was 'on little more than nodding terms with them, although I found it quite easy to talk to Bill Wyman, and Charlie and Shirley Watts were a delight to socialise with'.[13]

During another US tour, however, Andrew Oldham had had to talk Watts out of boarding a one-day flight back to London to surprise Shirley. There were to be other temptations to slip smoothly away into the skies and out of a frequently near-intolerable existence when a lighthearted mood might persist among the Stones for a few fiery-eyed miles before souring to cynical discontent, cliff-hanging silences and slanging matches. Hastily fed and superficially rested on arrival in another nondescript Holiday Inn, Ramada, Crest or Trust House, Charlie – who had an intensifying habit of sketching every hotel room in which he slept – was disturbed by the same man knocking at the door time and time again. 'Every time he opened it, the bloke was just rude to him,' added Mick Jagger. 'In the end, Charlie punched him on the nose. I was quite surprised as the fellow was about a foot taller than Charlie.'[14]

At the heart of most upsets on the road, however, was Brian Jones, now a poet of his own grief and the group's biggest liability. On one coast-to-coast trek, the Stones had honoured several dates as a four-piece after an immoderate combination of alcohol and amphetamines had taken an almost permanently addled Brian to a Chicago hospital – where, incidentally, only

Charlie and Bill bothered to visit his bedside. Afterwards, a doctor asked Charlie if he'd got a minute. It was like this: unless Brian pulled back from the abyss of booze and pills, he could be dead within a year.

Charlie passed his concern on to Brian's flatmate, Dave Thomson, who was more likely to persuade Jones to mend his ways than the doubtful company at his previous home. Brian's co-tenants there included Viv Prince, immortalised by television cameras when being escorted, inebriated, from a – grounded – Kiwi Airlines plane after an altercation with air hostess and pilot. Outstanding Pretty Things dates in Australasia were undertaken with Mitch Mitchell from Georgie Fame's Blue Flames, but New Zealand was sealed off to them for ever as if the Things were deadly microbes, threatening swift epidemic.

It was, however, administrative dithering that prevented The Pretty Things from participating directly in the 'British Invasion' of North America when, for a spell of several months in the mid-1960s, most of the UK's major post-Merseybeat pop stars – and many minor ones – made progress to varying extents in the uncharted United States and Canada. As well as The Beatles, the New World went almost as crackers about The Dave Clark Five, Freddie And The Dreamers and Herman's Hermits, outfits that adult America found a palatable compromise to an act of whom an Illinois newspaper wrote, 'You walk out of the amphitheatre after watching The Rolling Stones perform, and suddenly the Chicago stockyards smell good and clean by comparison.' [15]

In tacit acknowledgement, US immigration authorities temporarily refused visas for more Limey longhairs wishing to propagate their degenerate filth in Uncle Sam's fair land. Yet such was the preoccupation with British beat that a common complaint was that of Frank Zappa, then of Los Angeles' Soul Giants, 'If you didn't look like The Beatles or Stones, you didn't get hired.' [16] As well as the likes of The Byrds, The Walker Brothers and, most spectacularly, The Monkees, moulded less successfully to breadwinning UK specifications were such as The McCoys, ? And The Mysterions, The Standells, The Strangeloves and further local alternatives.

In the most unlikely back-street palais elsewhere, *circa* 1965, you'd come across many a parochial ensemble that had also reinvented itself as a British beat group – though stronger native characteristics would surface in time, and the most exotic instruments could supplement or replace guitar, bass and drum kit. An electric *saz* cropped up on 'Hard Work', a single by Turkey's Mogollar, while one of Uc Hurel played a twin-necked instrument – one neck for guitar, the other for *saz*. However, no 'Belly Dance Beat' or 'Black Sea Sound' ever took over the planet, but had an international pop scene not flowered, an enterprising talent scout from Britain or the USA might have found Istanbul or Ankara to be as vital a pop mecca as Liverpool and San Francisco.

To a more pragmatic end, there were instances of native talent checkmating UK originals. New Zealand's Ray Columbus And The Invaders issued a xerox of 'I Wanna Be Your Man', which outsold that by the Stones – who were on tour Down Under with a supporting cast that included Roy Orbison at the same time as a package containing Manfred Mann, The Kinks and The Honeycombs.

Epitomising the underlying good nature of British pop's most optimistic period – despite everything that makes pop groups what they are – was the Stones' half-serious proposal that Orbison – slaying audiences with his cowboy-operatic baritone – 'sing the worst record that I'd ever made, and I said I'd be happy to if they did the worst record they'd ever made. So I went on, and I figured that "Ooby Dooby" was the worst – so I sang it. Then they went on and I watched the performance, but they didn't do their worst record – but there was a little gathering afterwards and, in lieu of their not doing their worst record, they gave me a silver cigarette case. "From The Rolling Stones To Ooby Dooby", it's inscribed.'[17]

# 8 Houses

'Charlie's not really a Stone, is he? Mick, Keith and Brian, they're the big, bad Rolling Stones.'

*– Shirley Watts* [1]

Charlie and Shirley had bought their first house on 28 July 1965. Just outside Lewes, the Old Brewery was the seat of a 16th-century manor. It had the oak beams, the four-poster bed, the fireplace with space for half a tree to blaze in it, the library, the complete olde-worlde, countrified works. There were stables for Shirley's donkey and Energy, a racehorse; three cats and three collies roaming here and there; a nook given over to her collection of Victorian dolls, and a cranny for Charlie's mementoes of the US Civil War – rifles, revolvers, soldiers' uniforms and other artefacts purchased during stolen afternoon trips to Gettysburg and associated sites when the Stones were in the States.

The new residents were determined homebodies, who chose not to intervene much in parochial affairs. Nevertheless, the presence of a renowned addressee – one of those Rolling Stones – sent an electric thrill of mingled horror and joy throughout the entire postal district. The Old Brewery was exposed to the attention of a few fans, who'd sink into a languid daze induced by the fixity of gazing up the drive. However, commuting schoolchildren discovered that you could see more from the top deck of buses to and from Brighton where the Wattses ate at a favoured Chinese restaurant – certainly more favoured than one in Lewes after some unpleasantness when another diner's open insults, which embraced the phrase 'long-haired pansy', culminated with a scuffle into which Shirley was drawn too.

Charlie needed a little coaxing, but he and Shirley were also noticed frequenting West End clubland and attending concerts by bands such as The Who – after Charlie had been amused by guitarist Pete Townshend's blacked-out front teeth when the group were plugging 'I Can See For Miles' on *Top Of The Pops* – and Denny Laine's Electric String Band – the former singing guitarist with The Moody Blues fronting an amplified string quartet – at the Saville, a theatre owned by Brian Epstein. Following The Four Tops' appearance there on 13 November 1966, he hosted a party, among whose guests were various Beatles, Animals and Rolling Stones couples – including Shirley and a newly moustachioed Charlie. Sartorially, some of the others there were in transition from a post-Mod fad for Victorian militaria to flower power. 'I think I was the only rock star never to wear beads,' grinned Watts. 'I wish I could have done, but it never looked right on me.'[2]

On that same day, the *Sunday Telegraph*'s front page reported that two Beatles had approached a New York accountant called Allen Klein with a view to dealing him into their business affairs as the expiry date of their management contract with Epstein crept closer. Klein's reputation as the 'Robin Hood of pop' stood on his recouping of disregarded millions for his clients from seemingly iron-clad record company percentages. Through hovering over British pop as a hawk over a partridge nest, his administrative caress had come to encompass The Dave Clark Five, The Kinks and the uncut rubies – including The Animals and Herman's Hermits – that had been processed for the charts by freelance production whizz-kid Mickie Most. The Rolling Stones had also bitten, said Most, after they'd 'seen me driving around in the Rolls and owning a yacht, and started wondering where their money was going. Allen got them together and gave them money.'[3]

Exemplified by the pushing of Eric Easton and, eventually, Andrew Loog Oldham out of the Stones picture, Klein wasn't the most popular among record industry moguls but, wasting no time with small talk while driving hard and unrelenting bargains, 'he revolutionised the industry,' believed one accountant with no reason to love him. 'You've heard lots of terrible stories about him, most of which I concur with, but he was a tough American cookie, and he came over here and negotiated for the artists he was involved with.'[4] Paul McCartney had been particularly impressed by his wheedling of an unprecedentedly high advance from Decca for the Stones in 1965.

Allen was not, however, insensitive to shifts in the parameters of pop as the watershed year of 1967 neared. As trade figures were to signify, record labels would be committing more of their time and money to pop albums, a product that had been regarded, more often than not, as a testament to market pragmatism rather than quality – usually, a throwaway patchwork of tracks hinged on a hit 45. A new attitude had been heralded when groups that carried any weight began operating ambiguously with experimental fancies on LPs and, under pressure, tilting at the charts with the most trite or mainstream tracks – as did The Pretty Things with 'Private Sorrow' from *SF Sorrow*, unquestionably the first 'rock opera' (if, technically, a song cycle). 'What we were after,' elucidated Phil May, 'was an album that was one piece. That's why it had a story – the only way we could give it continuity.' Dick Taylor continued, 'EMI – probably because they didn't know what was going on – actually seemed quite willing to accept it – though they still took a single off it.'

Britain at large remained deaf to *SF Sorrow*, and its US release was delayed for nearly two years, prompting unfair accusations of plagiarism and jumping on the rock opera bandwagon. Pete Townshend was said to have had *SF Sorrow* on instant replay for nearly a week before getting to grips with *Tommy*. Moreover, it was not *SF Sorrow*, but The Beatles' more expensive and syncretic *Sgt Pepper's Lonely Hearts Club Band* that set the precedent for record companies underwriting further 'concept' albums; Decca entering the arena with The Rolling Stones' *Their Satanic Majesties Request.*

Aswarm with often jarring vignettes of music, it hinted at an aesthetic if wilfully uncommercial brilliance. It hinted too that its principal composers were under the influence of a drug far more mind-boggling – or 'psychedelic' – than any that had been common currency when first they'd touched the brittle fabric of fame. '*Satanic Majesties* was a very druggy period,' frowned Charlie, 'though not for me. I was never into drugs much at that time.'[5]

He had known all about marijuana since his student days in Harrow, but LSD – 'acid' – was on another narcotic plateau. He was 'terrified of the stuff. The psychedelic thing really messed a lot of people up, but it made people really talk to each other too.' In retrospect, he seemed to mourn not trying it just once for a possible glimpse, however chemically induced, at the eternal: 'maybe I'd have been a better person if I'd gone through all that.'[2]

Maybe not. LSD was contributory to the condensing inner chaos that, to Charlie's sadness, would lead to Brian Jones' exit from the Stones in 1969. The madness would subside for Mick and Keith, but not before the famous drugs bust in February 1967 at Richards' lodge in West Wittering. The police uncovered no LSD, but other substances found were enough to secure a jail sentence for both at West Sussex Quarter Sessions in June, albeit followed by dismissal on appeal within a week.

Though there were professional and personal interests at stake, Charlie and Shirley – like Ian and Cynthia Stewart, and Bill Wyman and Astrid, his steady girlfriend – could only spectate as the drama unfolded. 'The only thing I remember was Mick being in prison up the road to where I lived,' said Charlie. 'I went to visit him, but I couldn't get in.'[6]

'Just up the road' was now 'Hallard', still close to Lewes, but more secluded than The Old Brewery, and with a staff flat and cottage, a swimming pool, farm buildings and 34 acres of land. It was an improvement, but Watts was uneasy about relying on Allen Klein to see to the paying of the mortgage and expenses. With indecent haste, any open-handed conviviality around Allen's office desk had given way to probing suspicion about how much fiscal wool was being pulled over the Stones' eyes. By 1969, the wheels would be in motion for almost-but-not-quite phasing him out of their business concerns.

The slow mustering of legal forces to do so was not, however, the most urgent matter on Charlie's mind at the close of 1967 when flower power was supplanted by slouch-hatted, tailboard-riding Al Capone chic from the golden age of jazz. Shirley was in the final months of a pregnancy that would yield her and Charlie's only child, Serafina, born on 18 March 1968.

This coincided with a long period when The Rolling Stones had downed tools as a touring band for two years – from a date in Athens on 17 April 1967 to 7 November 1969 in Colorado. In between, the only 'live' stage appearances would be ten minutes at another *NME* Pollwinners Concert and the fabled memorial to Brian Jones – who drowned a month after leaving the group – at Hyde Park on 5 July 1969. Charlie was, therefore, able to give the baby more paternal attention than most – and his friends agreed that fatherhood suited him.

Serafina's progress might have been something to chat about with Mick, John Mayall, Ginger Baker and other attendees at Alexis Korner's 40th birthday celebrations in Bayswater on 19 April 1968. Ginger was then one of Cream, a 'supergroup' formed with Eric Clapton, formerly in Mayall's Bluesbreakers – notable for instrumentalists who went on to greater success. Clapton's replacement, Peter Green, founded Fleetwood Mac with two other Mayall men, drummer Mick Fleetwood (from The Cheynes) and bass player John McVie – and the next Mayall guitarist Mick Taylor would be where Brian Jones had once been when the Stones went back on the road again.

The third member of Cream was Jack Bruce, who'd been with Baker in The Graham Bond Organisation, essentially the Blues Incorporated-related trio augmented by guitarist John McLaughlin and then Dick Heckstall-Smith. However, after the issue of the outfit's *Sound Of '65* LP, Bruce quit to be a Bluesbreaker. A subsequent sojourn with Manfred Mann had him miming on *Top Of The Pops* to 1966 chart-topper 'Pretty Flamingo'.

With Steve Winwood, then of The Spencer Davis Group, and Eric Clapton, Jack Bruce was also in The Powerhouse, a sextet convened by Manfred Mann's singer Paul Jones and pianist Ben Palmer for a jam session after-hours in an otherwise deserted Marquee. Among extant tracks issued on a 1967 album, *What's Shakin'*, was 'Crossroads', which was to be in the repertoire of Cream – who, at the time of Alexis Korner's party, were in the odd position of being one of the biggest box-office draws in North America while planning an appositely titled album, *Goodbye*.

Not long after Cream disbanded in November 1969, Bruce joined John McLaughlin, Tony Williams and US guitarist Larry Coryell in Lifetime, a dissolving of outlines between jazz and rock. Meanwhile, Clapton and Baker had been reeled into Blind Faith, a lesser 'supergroup' than Cream, that lasted for just one tour of North America.

During this jaunt, an off-duty Clapton loafed around on rest days with the workmanlike support act, Delaney And Bonnie And Friends, made up mostly of a cabal of Los Angeles session musicians nicknamed 'the blue-eyed soul school'. From Eric's own pocket came the necessary outlay for the aggressively friendly Friends' European tour in 1969 – with himself as lead guitarist. After an age of anonymous studio drudgery, some soon ascertained that taking up British residency and breathing the air round Clapton – and his pals in the Stones and the fragmenting

Beatles – was a springboard to, if not fame, then a stronger negotiating stance for more extortionate session fees.

When introduced, Charlie Watts was overwhelmed by the Friends' freewheeling exuberance. Their detailing of the previous night's carnal shenanigans and stimulant intake could prove monotonous, but otherwise they were good company. In reciprocation, Charlie was loud once more in praise of Jim Gordon, now their drummer.[7] Watts had also scraped acquaintance previously with Gordon's rapid successor, Jim Keltner, the former Gary Lewis Playboy – who was not so openly on the make, and was the Friend with whom Charlie felt most at ease.

Watts was also flattered to be requested to help out on an eponymous solo album by another Friend, Leon Russell, whose perpetual on-stage top hat and garnering of further assistance from George Harrison, Ringo Starr, Bill Wyman, Steve Winwood and other British names that would look grand in the LP's sleeve credits, were symptomatic of 'in-crowd' acknowledgement that he was the epitome of the smug sexism and 'funky' rhythmic jitter of the interchangeable Delaney And Bonnie 'super sidemen' who, crowed their saxophonist, 'went on to back all the players that really do have a lot of influence'.[8]

Considerably more prestigious that aiding Russell was Charlie's part in albums recorded in London by Howlin' Wolf and another revered bluesman in the late afternoon of his life, BB King. Since the resurgence of interest in the blues in the late 1960s – the 'blues boom' – they had been advised to gear their music to a wider forum by reprising their best-known numbers with some of the renowned white musicians they had inspired. Wolf, however, had been disappointed with the US band used for the first venture in this vein, 1969's *This Is Howlin' Wolf's New Album*..., but, issued on the Rolling Stones' own label, 1971's *London Sessions* was more than satisfactory as his guttural bass-baritone ground out the lyrics of 'Little Red Rooster',[9] 'Sitting

On Top Of The World' and all the rest of them to accompaniment by producer Glyn Johns' British volunteers – Charlie, Bill, Steve, Eric, all the usual shower – effusive with deferential humour and glad co-operation.

Since the less absolute of Brian's departures, the atmosphere had been as genial during the recording of the first single with Mick Taylor, 'Honky Tonk Women'. It seemed that no harm had been done by the upheaval as it tramped a well-trodden path to Number One on both sides of the Atlantic. It was produced by Jimmy Miller, a New Yorker who'd been headhunted by The Spencer Davis Group and then Steve Winwood's next outfit, Traffic.

Miller was also a drummer of such proficiency that it provoked no friction with Watts when he took over at the kit on magniloquent 'You Can't Always Get What You Want', B-side of 'Honky Tonk Women' – on which Miller tapped a cowbell in counterpoint to a stomping and not-quite-medium-tempo Watts introit. If technically awry – and plus a tempo that had all but doubled in speed by the final chorus[10] – it went unchanged to the pressing plant for much the same reasons as The Dave Clark Five's percussion-driven 'Bits And Pieces' in 1964. 'At the beginning, I was slightly behind,' confessed Clark, 'but it worked. It was also supposed to have eight foot stomps in each break, but in one of them, there were only seven and a half. I kept it that way because it had energy. It would have been wrong to go back and re-record it. Sometimes you make mistakes, and out of them, good things happen.'[11]

Naturally, 'Honky Tonk Women' was among principal crowd-pleasers when the group resumed touring with a sixth expedition to North America. 'Suddenly, shows were incredibly long,' noticed Charlie, 'and there would be no audience reaction until after the number. Then everyone went mad.'[12]

The comeback finished on a sour note at a free open-air concert at Altamont Speedway near Livermore, California. The

20-mile traffic jams fanning out in all directions and the shortage of portable toilets were the least of it. Portrayed by tabloid and broadsheet as a pop hybrid of the Black Hole of Calcutta and the Hillsborough disaster, it left four dead, one of them murdered and with members of a chapter of the Hell's Angels the chief suspects. 'It was badly organised,' understated Charlie Watts. 'You couldn't really see the audience. All you could see was the Angels, who were near us, protecting us. The thing that stuck in my mind was somebody being hit on the head with a billiard cue, and seeing a motorbike fall over in front of the stage, and the guy whose motorbike it was complaining.'[6]

# 9 Jamming

'Charlie visited the studio when we were doing the Renaissance album. We had a chat about drums, and he seemed a very down-to-earth guy.'

*– Jim McCarty*

On 11 October 2003, The Pretty Things were performing in a hall designed for championship sport in Helmond, Holland. They shared the bill with a Dutch Joe Cocker tribute band – and Dave Berry, maker of 1965's 'This Strange Effect', the biggest-selling single in the country's history. This was the finale of his act, but, to Dick Taylor, Dave's periodic references to the era of his optimum impact were enough to please a receptive audience. Indeed, his mere yelling of 'The '60s!' into the microphone always sparked off an orgy of delighted cheering.

Just as the third millennium began not on New Year's Day 2000, but 11 September 2001, so the buoyant optimism of the decade known as the swinging '60s, pop's turbulent adolescence, had been over psychologically long before 31 December 1969 – or, for that matter, earlier in the month with Altamont, viewed from the distance of years as the darker of the twin climaxes of hippy culture. The other was when another half-million North Americans had endured rain-drenched Woodstock in August.

Nearly all the old heroes had gone down. The Yardbirds, The Small Faces, The Animals, The Byrds, The Spencer Davis Group, The Dave Clark Five, Manfred Mann, Jefferson Airplane, The Zombies and, of course, The Beatles had all either disintegrated or were about to disintegrate, leaving a residue of mostly tedious splinter groups, supergroups and solo performers to add to a growing pile. The Yardbirds, for instance, had split into two contrasting factions: Led Zeppelin, soon to be stereotyped as the ultimate heavy metal outfit, and Renaissance, whose maiden album embraced folk, *musique concrete* and the post-serialist tonalities of Ligeti and Penderecki. Many 1960s acts were to reform, but such a possibility was denied The Jimi Hendrix Experience after the death of its leader – though The Doors struggled on for a while without their late focal point, Jim Morrison.

Without going into many more distressing details, the 1970s began as a re-run of 1967 without colour, daring, humour or, arguably, originality. *The* hit song of 1970 was Free's 'All Right Now', which had appropriated the salient points of 'Honky Tonk Women' – while, beyond *Top Of The Pops*, were album-enhancing 45s by Humble Pie, Man, Budgie, Mountain and other 'heavy' ensembles, who appealed to male consumers grown lately to man's estate.

Jazz-rock was in favour with them too. Its truest home was the USA, which abounded with the ilk of Weather Report, Return To Forever, The Jazz Crusaders and oldest-teenager-in-the-business Miles Davis, who were often castigated for their employment of synthesisers and similarly state-of-the-art keyboards that, no matter how cleverly utilised, seemed impassive and gutless against the potentially more thrilling margin of error with 'real' instruments.

Theoretically, Britain had entered the jazz-rock lists on disc as long ago as *The Five Faces Of Manfred Mann* and, also in 1964, Georgie Fame's *R&B At The Flamingo* – not to mention the offerings of, say, The Sheffields, The Artwoods and The Mark Leeman Five. Now that the style had been categorised with a designated name, however, it spawned respectable exponents who, unlike Weather Report, Return To Forever *et al*, preferred instinct to technique – among them East Of Eden, Colosseum, half of Lifetime and, on the rebound from a sojourn with Miles Davis, John McLaughlin and his Mahavishnu Orchestra.

Roaming the kingdom's furthest reaches of jazz-rock – or jazz-something – were The People Band, an entity connected to both The Battered Ornaments – unfortunates who'd been booed venomously during a spot just before the Stones at Hyde Park – and North London's avant-garde theatre group, The People Show, who were resident in one of the Arts Laboratories that had come into being *circa* 1967, and had muddled on, encouraging all manner of artists to make use of its workshop ambience.

Whenever The People Band ventured beyond this underground security, a minority absorbed their freeform recitals in a knowing, nodding sort of way, while blocking out the impure thought in the tacit question, 'How could anyone like this stuff?' prior to clapping politely when it ceased, this 'spontaneous music' that others enjoyed for 'the wrong reasons' rather than comprehending with pitying superiority that the more effort needed to appreciate it, the more 'artistic' it must be.

Though often cynosures of an unnerving stare from what looked like a gigantic photograph of silent and undemonstrative onlookers, The People Band's core personnel was distinguished after a retrospective fashion, containing as it did drummer Rob Tait – to be heard on albums by Kevin Ayers, Gong, Dick Heckstall-Smith and Vinegar Joe – and keyboard player Charlie Hart, who was to work with Ronnie Lane of the once and future Small Faces, The Who's Pete Townshend and, via art school pal Ian Dury, Wreckless Eric – while Roger Potter and George Kahn, respectively on bass and woodwinds, were ever present session players in London. Guest musicians on the Band's 1970 LP included saxophonist Lyn Dobson, once of Manfred Mann and, more recently, Soft Machine, and Mike Figgis, who cut his teeth as trumpeter in Newcastle soul band The Gas Board, with whom Bryan Ferry had been awaiting his destiny with Roxy Music.

Finally, there was Charlie Watts, who not only drummed on the album, but produced it. He was advantaged by a comprehensive shadowing of studio methodology since Glyn Johns taped the Stones at IBC in early 1963. Recognised as a proficient engineer too – and, when available, a discreetly in-demand one – Charlie's instructions at the console were now dotted with erudite jargon as he decreed theoretical apportionment of trackage, shortlisting of devices and effects, and general operational definition, while getting down to specifics with learned procrastinations over, perhaps, degree of reverberation overspill allowable on Kahn's flute.

Regardless of intrinsic content – and it was the sound at any given moment that counted more than the six individual excerpts from a continuous performance – The People Band's LP had breadth of sonic expression that, if confident and clean, didn't detract from the forceful gusto. Neither was it pat, dovetailed and American with neatly executed solos floating effortlessly over layers of treated sound. [1]

Crude-but-effectiveness was more pronounced, however, on budget-priced *Jamming With Edward*, the fourth album to be released by Rolling Stones Records, the label created as part of the deal with Atlantic after Decca had been seen off with 1970's *Get Yer Ya-Yas Out*, an in-concert bash taped at Madison Square Gardens on the Altamont tour. Though it wasn't as onerous a public office on his group's behalf as singer Roger Daltrey's self-immersion into a bath of baked beans for the cover of *The Who Sell Out*, Charlie permitted himself to be photographed for *Get Yer Ya-Yas Out*'s front cover, prancing gleefully before a backdrop of a flat countryside landscape, top-hatted and with an electric guitar in either hand. Bearing Bill Wyman's four-string, a bass drum and a floor tom-tom, a donkey peers indifferently at him.

While only the most hooked Stones devotee might have bothered to decipher this symbolism – if that's what it was – *Get*

*Yer Ya-Yas Out* topped the domestic chart and lingered for weeks in the US Top Ten that autumn. Mick's 'Charlie's good tonight, isn't he?' comment during the continuity survived the editing, though the drummer himself was still becoming accustomed to the lengthy and uproarious tribal gatherings that were post-psychedelic rock extravaganzas. As Charlie had noticed already, 'rock bands' – not pop groups – no longer thought that a ten-minute slot on something-for-everybody scream-circuit packages was sufficient any more. The 50 vinyl minutes of *Get Yer Ya-Yas Out* had been pruned down from two nights, each with the Stones spending well over twice that time on stage each time.

Among remaindered items were 'Prodigal Son', virtually a Jagger–Richards duet, because on-stage silences and pianissimos were undercut by a ceaseless barrage of stamping, whistling, discomforted snarls and, worst of all, bawled requests for the good old good ones like '19th Nervous Breakdown', 'Paint It Black', anything loud.

Such occupational irritations weren't peculiar to the Stones. Maddened by noise and body pressure, one hot-headed riot squad had been so goaded by Ginger Baker's reprimands for their arbitrary manhandling of fans during Blind Faith's US tour in 1969, that the now so-called 'high priest of percussion'[2] himself was a recipient of their punches and kicks. Was Baker berating the uniforms that guarded him as the supergroup's initial low volume led dismayed bottles, cans and even plates of food to be hurled stagewards? On another occasion, homely, receding Ginger was scragged behind his kit by maverick souvenir hunters who fled with his sticks as the tardy cops waded in.

The Stones' security was too tight for Charlie to be victim of such undignified assault. The most tender nerves prodded by *Get Yer Ya-Yas Out* were a continued assimilation of what good had come from the most harrowing public journey of his – and the others' – career and, more pragmatically, 'When they miked drums up, it became a whole other world – but they can't take away the character you develop in your relationship between the cymbal and the snare drum. Great players have that, but when you get somebody else's version, when you get a guy mixing you, it's very loud but flat. You wouldn't need that with Kenny Clarke.'[3]

Yet he had developed a swift acceptance of both this and toiling behind his kit in North America's baseball parks and concrete coliseums. 'I'm not resigned to my position as a frustrated jazz musician or anything,' he shrugged. 'This is what I do – and I don't consider myself anything else.'[4]

The new regime, its attendant increase in on-stage volume and the advent of monitor speakers also brought to the fore the idiosyncrasies of the Stones' approach to corporate rhythm. The concept of the guitarists and singer being controlled *en bloc* by tempos defined by bass and drums had always been a misnomer – as it was in other famous groups. 'It's the way I place the lyric on the beat,' was vocalist Reg Presley's assessment of how it was with his Troggs. 'Ronnie [Bond] hits his snare a fraction behind, and Chris [Britton]'s guitar is somewhere in between. There's such a closeness in how that happens, a matter of a split second.'[5]

In the Stones' case, it had boiled down to an interaction hinged on the good/bad rawness of Keith Richards' chord-slashing, compulsively exquisite even to more proficient guitarists who could hear what was technically askew. Bill Wyman's elucidation is worth quoting at length: 'Our band does not follow the drummer. Our drummer follows the rhythm guitarist. Immediately, you've got something like a one-hundredth of a second delay between the guitar and Charlie's lovely drumming. On-stage, you have to follow Keith. You have no way of not following him. With Charlie following Keith, you have that very minute delay. The net result is that loose type of pulse that goes between Keith, Charlie and me.'[6]

'Keith knows in general that we're following him, so he doesn't care if he changes the beat around or isn't really aware of it. He'll drop a half- or quarter-bar somewhere, and suddenly Charlie's playing on the beat instead of the backbeat. He'll be so surprised, and be very uptight to get back in, because it's very hard for a drummer to swap the beat, especially on the intros. He's got monitors, but, if you're not hearing too well with the screaming crowds, its very difficult to hear the accents, the difference between the soft and hard strokes. The problem is that he's often totally unaware that he's on the wrong beat, and he shuts his eyes and he's gone. Someone has to go up and kick the cymbal – but I think that's a little of the charm of the Stones.'[4]

Richards had failed to work his magic at one session for the transitional *Let It Bleed* album – to which both Mick Taylor and Brian Jones contributed – in May 1969. It was one of those nights when jamming consumed more time than usual as late arrivals set up their gear and console boffins twiddled. Nothing was seen of Keith for the entire time that Charlie, Mick, Bill and two auxiliary players were there. Nevertheless, it was thought prudent to keep the tape rolling so that edited highlights – if that is the word – could be cobbled together for release nearly three years later as *Jamming With Edward*. While Jagger managed a slightly muted revival of an Elmore James blues, the proceedings were dominated by the catalytic familiars, namely Nicky Hopkins – to the fore on 'Highland Fling', titled for its aptly Hibernian pentatonic overtones on piano – and Ry Cooder, Los Angeles-born bottleneck guitar exponent and music archivist.

'Blow With Ry' was cast adrift on the vinyl oceans as a German single in 1969, but, in common with 'Edward's Thrump Up', 'Boudoir Stomp' and the rest of *Jamming With Edward*, the clouds parting on the gods at play revealed little more remarkable than any idle studio crew's wanderings after one of them kicks off an extemporisation that lives principally in its riff. Nevertheless, it wasn't entirely an immortalisation of the participants' own arrogance as it made for cheaper and far less tedious listening than George Harrison's similarly motivated 'Apple Jam' third of 1970's *All Things Must Pass* triple album.

Furthermore, it had been a long time since 'I Do Like To See Me On The B-Side', and *Jamming With Edward* earned Charlie a couple more rare composing credits. Compared to his share in income for record sales and the budgetary receptacle for all net profits from concerts, this meant but pin-money at a juncture when much was rotten financially in the state of the Stones. Each member had been challenged with what was a sky-high tax bill 30 inflationary years ago. It had snowballed over seven years of international stardom. Burdensome Inland Revenue demands on high earners in a high-risk business were also to drive Dave Clark into a year's fiscal exile in California, Maurice Gibb of The Bee Gees to the Isle of Man, Led Zeppelin to Guernsey and then Switzerland, and Reg Presley to sell his grand self-built mansion in Hampshire's open countryside for an unostentatious house along one of Andover's main suburban thoroughfares.

Though *persona non grata* now, Allen Klein had, like he'd said he would, made the Stones a fortune from increased record company percentages, an accounting system that had eradicated the smallest petty-cash fiddles and the repair of the dam that had burst on wasteful organisational tributaries – but where was that fortune now? Why weren't their present financial advisers confident that a search for plausible avenues for rebate or playing for time would be successful?

The answer was that far too little had been set aside for such an unthinkable catastrophe. A lackadaisical assumption that they had wealth beyond calculation now surrendered to circular and half-understood discussions filled with phrases like 'convertible debenture' and 'tax concession', and much probing about how this figure had been calculated and why so-and-so had been granted that franchise. With terrifying sureness, it would leave Charlie trying to put a brave face on the realisation that the family had either to move to a humbler home in England or, with Mick as chief advocate, migrate *sur le continent* until the dust settled.

# 10  Exile

'If Charlie don't get into it, then I haven't written
something that the Stones can get a groove going on.'
                                    *– Keith Richards*[1]

Through a combination of Jagger's persistence and the weariness
they all felt about the ugly situation, the Stones uprooted to the
Côte d'Azure after what was publicised as a 'farewell' tour of
Britain, starting at Newcastle City Hall on 4 March 1971. The
final date was at the capital's barn-like Roundhouse where,
afterwards, Jim Gordon and Jim Keltner, still at large in London,
nattered with proud cordiality to Charlie. Indeed, both Keltner
and Watts had assisted on recent sessions for the jazzy *Feel Your
Groove* by Ben Sidran, a singing pianist from Wisconsin, who
had passed through the ranks of The Steve Miller Band prior to
studying at the University of Sussex.

Charlie and Shirley had resigned themselves to the
inevitability of three-year-old Serafina's formal education
commencing in the south of France where, with their
customary pragmatism, they had been inspecting suitable
properties on the market since the previous autumn. While the
other Stones were still looking, the Watts family were settling
into a farmhouse in Provence, half-hidden by woodland and
set in the foothills of the Cevennes and within the tributary pull
of the Loire and the hinterland of Marseilles – though only the
*diddley-dum-clickety-clack* of a far-distant train interrupted
the rustic calm.

The presence of a Rolling Stone there was profoundly unsettling for a village Socrates, used to being centre of attention when holding forth on a cafe terrace. He'd be completely ignored by his audience, and would fall silent himself when the unfamiliar car's engine died in the sun-drenched square, and the renowned newcomer and his *femme* climbed out for the ritual of shopping for groceries. Such an excursion was complicated by Shirley having to motor from their new home along twisty lanes, followed by potential language and currency misunderstandings at the checkout, especially as the local dialect was markedly different from Shirley's schoolgirl French. Nevertheless, the stay overseas was to be agreeable enough, and disturbed by but one prominent mishap.

On 3 June in Nice, *Madame* Watts had been threading slowly through a customs area resounding with jack-in-office incivility and too many fibres of red tape. Harassed to breaking point, Shirley – so a magistrate would be informed – marinated the air with curses and physically attacked one singularly intransigent official before boarding a flight to London. Pop star's wife or not, she wasn't above the law, and a custodial sentence was in order on top of a small fine. Fortunately for Shirley, she was still in England when the case came up, but the ordained six months in a foreign jail hung over her for two months until reduced on appeal to a suspended 15 days.

The experience faded and, while there was a tendency to view Lewes through a rosy haze, life returned not to normal exactly, but to the relocated domestic routine broken by Charlie's necessary journeys beyond the rutted trackways and seas of breeze-blown yellow grass to Keith's Mediterranean coastal abode where the basement had been converted into a studio for the purpose of recording basic tracks for what would turn out to be the Stones' sole double album, *Exile On Main Street*, throughout a typically hot summer in the region.

Shuttered underground on a flaming July afternoon in the

newly installed drum isolation booth, his forehead bestowed with pinpricks of sweat, his headphoned ears like mildly braised chops, Charlie thumped out take after rejected take, emerging occasionally to listen hard to a playback amid the spools and blinking dials or plunge into one of the occasional contretemps that scaled such a height of stand-up vexation and cross-purpose that underlings and hirelings – including two female backing vocalists – would slope off for embarrassed coffee breaks while defiance, hesitation, defiance again and final agreement chased across the face of Jimmy Miller or, more frequently, Keith, *Exile On Main Street*'s principal driving force.

While each track began to assume sharper definition, the old ennui manifested itself in Charlie's just hovering around during some monotonous mechanical process at the desk or constant re-tapings of some minor guitar overdub. He came to know by sight individual sweet wrappers, and note their day-to-day journeyings up and down a ledge, where an empty whisky bottle of Keith's might also remain for weeks next to a discarded swab-stick made grubby from cleaning tape heads.

Yet Charlie Watts had stumbled upon ever deeper reserves of patience as the years had passed: 'When we're recording, it's not a question of getting it over quickly. It's getting a take which the majority likes. This tends to take longer than it did when we first started. The consolation is that these days, our records sound so much better.

'As far as I'm concerned, once I've done my bit, there's nothing else for me to do except hang about in the studio. It's OK if the boys have brought some people in to do overdubs or the girls are doing a back-up vocal track. Otherwise, it's just boring.'[2]

Like it was when Jimmy Miller took over on 'You Can't Always Get What You Want'. Charlie had long been sure enough of his position within the Stones to be quite amenable to similar corner-cutting, such as Kenney Jones of The Faces – the Woodstock Generation's very own Brian Poole And The

Tremeloes – beating the skins on 'It's Only Rock 'n' Roll (But I Like It)', the title song and spin-off hit single from the next album but one after *Exile On Main Street*. It would be knocked together at the London home studio of Faces guitarist Ron Wood before he superseded Mick Taylor in the Stones – and, following Keith Moon's sudden death in 1978, Kenney Jones joined The Who.

As he'd been within earshot of the other Stones for every working day since God knows when, he felt the relief of a day off and the acceptance of easy money when Kenney's contribution passed muster, and Charlie wasn't required to layer his own drumming on to the invested rhythm and tempo of 'It's Only Rock 'n' Roll'. Conversely, how refreshing it had been to undertake extramural projects such as assisting on Howlin' Wolf's *London Revisited* earlier in 1974 and, the previous year, on Alexis Korner's 1973 album, *Bootleg Him*, with other representatives from assorted trackways of his old boss's professional life, among them Dick Heckstall-Smith, Herbie Goins, Ginger Baker, Graham Bond,[3] Jack Bruce, Andy Fraser and Paul Rodgers of Free – which owed its very name to Korner – and Robert Plant, yet another protégé. He had performed in a duo with Alexis before throwing in his lot with Led Zeppelin in 1969 with his pal, drummer John Bonham, who put his back into a truculent frenzy of cross-patterns and ringing silverware in 'Moby Dick', the number that would frame a drum solo on 1970's *Led Zeppelin II* – and one that could last up to 30 minutes on the boards.

With Plant's lung power on a par with instrumental sound-pictures of Genghis Khan carnage from the other three members, Led Zeppelin had soon filled the market void left by the defunct Cream more effectively than the short-lived Blind Faith. Snow-blinded acclaim for their deafening heads-down-no-nonsense rock on stage was accompanied by turmoil as, typified by attendance by nearly 60,000 in an exposition centre in Tampa,

Florida, Led Zeppelin broke box-office records held previously not only by Cream, but also The Beatles and, for a while, The Rolling Stones.

Led Zeppelin were taking the USA for every cent they could get through a hectic succession of tours with manager Peter Grant demanding and receiving up to 90 per cent of gross receipts for every show. A decent interval after Altamont, no time was better for another Rolling Stones US barnstormer – plus some European dates, even if none of these could accommodate the same tens of thousands in one go. With appetites whetted by 'Tumbling Dice', a recent 45, in *Billboard*'s spring Top Ten, and the imminent release of million-selling *Exile On Main Street*, Uncle Sam's pop-pickers were awaiting a carnival of greater magnitude than even Led Zeppelin.

Dollars danced before the gleaming eyes of the Stones and their investors as telephones rang with merchandising deals, advances against takings, and estimates spewed out at a second's notice by entrepreneurs yelling 'Klondike!' Within days, a two-month trek across North America was in place for summer 1972. The asking prices per concert were reported to be comparable to the million greenbacks pocketed by David Bowie for one notable US recital in the consequent fatter decade.

As these blizzards of notes subsided into wads, market research showed that loud had become louder and then loudest. Present at Madison Square Garden for a Zeppelin blitzkrieg, ex-Yardbird Chris Dreja remembered the volume from the PA system and flat-out amplifiers 'literally moving the concrete in front of 50,000 people. Having not been to many such events since The Yardbirds, it completely freaked me out.'

Well, the Stones could equal that – and the limousines, private jets, portable stage, backstage area theoretically as impenetrable as Howard Hughes' Las Vegas penthouse, and the general protective bubble amid the howling publicity and celebrity guest lists. They could also match the 'festival seating', which at many venues often meant 'no seating' – so when the stadium doors were flung open, everyone with the same-priced tickets grappled for a clear vantage point.

In one of pop's slow moments, there were few other overt focuses of adoration in the States in mid-1972, nothing hysterical or outrageous. With David Bowie only a marginal success then, glam rock was no more than a trace element in the *Hot 100*. While precedents were yet to be forged by the likes of The Ramones in New York's twilight zone and The Sex Pistols' exploratory rehearsals in London, cheap spirits, Mandrax, headbanging and streaking were among desperate diversions that were catching on as 1973 loomed.

The sub-Zeppelin headlining act delivering the expected high-energy blues-plagiarised brutality was merely an excuse for buddies to get smashed out of their brains together after heading for the toilets during the support act to partake of various illegal drugs on offer. Blood splattered a water-closet ceiling where someone had been shooting up heroin inexpertly. Back in the arena, urine-filled beer cans would be hurled stagewards if the band didn't boogie. Few of these odious projectiles, however, landed within the spotlight's glare, where matchstick figures with double drum kits and V-shaped electric guitars cavorted, making a gradually more distant noise, and completely oblivious to the squalor before them.

When the Stones' juggernaut shifted out of neutral, a gang rape was reported after a second house somewhere on the east coast was kept waiting beyond midnight. In Vancouver, 2,000 would-be gatecrashers were beaten back by police. Further injuries and arrests were blamed on hundreds of forged tickets in Albuquerque and Montreal – where a bottle aimed at Jagger found its mark. Some kind of punch-up on Rhode Island involving him, Keith and a couple of journalists had ended with a pending court hearing. Everything was different, everything was the same – but worse.

Ian Stewart had strolled pensively round another abused amphitheatre somewhere else in the midwest. It was now deserted but for a bulldozer scooping residual tons of broken bottles, cigarette packets, discarded garments and other litter left by the rabble.

The tour had been a sell-out, affirming the group's resonance as both figureheads and grey eminences of late-20th-century pop, but, forgetting the glowing reviews and the upward curves on profit graphs, where did Ian's Rolling Stones belong in all this? You'd take a good book to kill time, but, after endless centuries of self-loathing, it'd occur to you that you'd scarcely glanced at it the whole trip. Travel didn't broaden the mind, but brought souvenirs without wisdom and fatigue without stimulation – unless you counted Charlie's chats with a chef he'd met in Chicago about when this new-found friend was employed as a chauffeur by various city gangsters during the Prohibition era.

Mick Taylor had had almost enough and, if one of these quiet, shy blokes who kept himself to himself, he would be marshalling his words and daring a resignation speech within a year. Sitting quietly in the corner at some post-concert party or other, he, Stewart and Watts drank in a scene not so much *Satyricon* as a BBC play mock-up of an imagined pop group drugs-and-sex orgy. In a haze of marijuana smoke, pushers, groupies, gold-diggers, socialites and other loud-mouthed periphery competed to actuate inane dialogue with Jagger while, over on a makeshift stage, one of the horn section was life-and-soul of an interminable blues jam.

Mention of The Rolling Stones on the road in the early 1970s still brings out strange tales of what people claim they saw and heard. Certain eye-stretching rumours of narcotic-fuelled escapades and weird sex behind closed doors in hotel suites were founded in hard fact, but many other antics later attributed to the principals had taken place under the alibi of the stage act, were improved with age or were originated by others in the entourage, who, if admirable young men in many ways, had their quota of young men's vices.

With libidinous admirers aspiring to an orgasm at the thrust of a *bona fide* Rolling Stone, advantages were taken of the casual and unchallenging sexual gratification procurable from pulchritudinous and often notorious females practised at evading the most stringent security barricades to impose themselves on well-known musicians. On Led Zeppelin's last coast-to-coast excursion, Robert Plant had been cited in one US journal as 'a self-satisfied sexual gourmet'. This may have been as much of a slur on his good name as whispers that Jimmy Page, though a 'perfect gentleman' to supergroupie, Bebe Buell, was even more of a Lothario on the road than Plant.[4]

Stray mutterings about the Stones party's erotic antics filtered via gossip columns and word of mouth to Shirley Watts in another time zone. Fêted wherever they went, the most debauched Roman emperor might never have had it so good. Yet Charlie in particular was able to make light of the gradually more mythical aura of sexual malpractice that some insisted they could sense emanating from the Stones. 'Does your wife know you're here?' he joked when spying Jim Keltner nattering with Keith Richards along some backstage corridor.[5] 'I wouldn't want my wife associating with us', was his Groucho Marx-esque quip at hearsay about a ship-in-the-night affair between one of his colleagues and the with-it wife of Canada's Prime Minister.[2]

While she recalled her spouse's period as an unattached London bachelor *circa* 1963, Shirley was convinced that Charlie had never been tempted into so much as a one-night stand while in a different hemisphere often for months at a stretch. Indeed, disappointed girls with erotic designs on him envied Shirley for hooking such a well-heeled rock idol of a man who proffered conversation as an alternative to any dalliance in the romantic seclusion of, say, a backstage broom cupboard.

There is no evidence whatsoever that Charlie was ever unfaithful to his wife at any point during one of showbusiness's longest-lasting marriages, despite 'a lot of separation', sighed Shirley. 'A band like The Rolling Stones is more demanding than another woman. You have to learn how to cope with it – but you can't hang around someone's neck and always be with them. Of course, I've had fears about groupies, but I don't worry any more. I trust him.'[6]

# 11  Boogie

'It was Charlie's call. It was his name that made all the difference.'

*– Bob Hall*[1]

The Stones' financial position was healthy enough by 1973 for individuals to consider living in England again. Certainly, the group was now above the tour-album-tour sandwiches incumbent upon poorer stars, and could wait until they felt like making a new album or taking to the road again – as exemplified by a rejection of *105 per cent* (!) of the gross take for a single concert at Lincoln's Drill Hall on 16 June 1973. Like Elvis Presley, Bob Dylan and Frank Zappa, the Stones were racking up far heftier sales in the decade after they'd made their most prominent mark. These included repackagings and previously unissued scrapings from the Decca archives, nearly all of them compiled with a pronounced pre-Mick Taylor bias, thus fuelling the argument that whatever the Stones got up to in the years left to them was barely relevant.

Nevertheless, chart entries did not yet depend upon commercial viability. The Stones were assured, more often than not, of at least a minor hit with whatever was released under their name. Even 'Happy' – with Keith Richards on lead vocals – from the already successful *Exile On Main Street*, spent five weeks in the US Top 30, while Decca's exhumation of a nine-year-old version of 'Out Of Time', an *Aftermath* opus, was to harry the lower reaches of the UK Top 50 in 1975.

Other swinging '60s behemoths, such as The Searchers and Wayne Fontana, were embarking on the first 'British Invasion' nostalgia tours of the States, and discovering that all that fans, old and new, wanted were the sounds of yesteryear. Yet the Stones proved able to counterpoise raising the roof with 'Satisfaction', 'Jumpin' Jack Flash' *et al* and earning more considered ovations for their most recent output when materialising like ghosts from the recent past – and with no current album to promote – in Australasia in early 1973 and then criss-crossing Europe from summer into autumn.

In between such expeditions, Charlie Watts was sighted as often as the Loch Ness Monster: backstage at the Hammersmith Odeon on 7 June 1973 after a show by Wings, Paul McCartney's new outfit; clattering fork on plate in a Montparnasse restaurant; joining Georgie Fame and Eric Clapton in an *ad hoc* group at Glyn Johns' wedding reception; or in Soho, sporting a crew-cut and thumbing through scuffed wares in a vintage record shop that specialised in jazz. Meanwhile, vibrantly gregarious Mick Jagger seemed to be an ever-present guest at every high-society shindig, club opening, after-dinner laudation and big-names-in-good-cause charity function. 'I'd hate to be Mick,' confessed Charlie. 'I'm glad to say he's promoted himself in that direction – always in the magazines – because it helps us. It's great for me because I'd never do that. I hate that sort of thing.'[2]

However wide the chasm between Watts' and Jagger's social and recreational interests, artistic outlines dissolved when the two collaborated with the stage designer for the summer 1975 tour of 'the Americas' (and the group's first with Ron Wood). The idea was to emulate the pageant of sunrise via the unfolding of a huge metal lotus flower containing the five Stones – plus a conga player, Ollie Brown, sharing Charlie's podium – after they pitched into an opening 'Honky Tonk Women' segued from a taped percussion item.

With the spooky deliberation of a dream's slow motion, the hydraulically operated petals would be fully flattened on the stage floor and extended like cat-walks into the crowd by the song's last cadence. Thanks to the planned and specific positioning of this spectacle in a given venue and overhead speakers hoisted on gantries like oil derricks, when had the Stones ever been seen so well or heard so clearly?

The enlistment of a hand-drummer had been at Charlie's instigation – as had the strategy of launching the tour not with a run-of-the-mill press conference, but a flat-bed lorry – with attached electricity generator – to be driven with majestic slowness down Fifth Avenue, New York's busiest thoroughfare. On the back, the Stones would smash out a protracted and traffic-jamming 'Brown Sugar', while the upper windows of offices and department stores filled to watch a swelling trail of starstruck pedestrians clotting the pavements, and the exhaust pipes of taxis belching out their anger at the delay. 'The old jazz bands used to do it,' Charlie had explained, 'to publicise their gigs for the evening.'[3]

Such a carnival atmosphere belied an episode during rehearsals in a house owned by Andy Warhol in upstate New York when, according to Ron Wood, Charlie had had a 'mild flip-out'[3] because Mick kicked his drum kit. None the less, during his ordained introductions of the other personnel, Jagger was beaming when the adulation of the hordes was directed towards Charlie, and the tour passed with far less incident and amassed more profit than any other thus far. Moreover, the consensus was that the Stones had put up a far better show than rival attractions like George Harrison, whose trek round the sub-continent the previous autumn had been marred by his persistent laryngitis, taking of unpardonable lyrical liberties and unappealing reinventions such as a 'My Sweet Lord' at breakneck speed.

There'd been a sneaky and initially unrecognisably mordant 'Satisfaction' recently, but the Stones seemed to be coming to terms with both their past and present situations with the realisation that all an act still intact from the 1960s needed to do to please the crowd was to be an archetypal unit of its own, spanning every familiar trackway of its professional career – the timeless hits, the changes of image, the bandwagons jumped. Yet giving 'em, maybe, 'If You Can't Rock Me' from *It's Only Rock 'N' Roll* was not regarded as an indulgence, an obligatory lull requiring a more subdued reaction than that for when 'Brown Sugar' or 'Tumbling Dice' makes everything all right again.

Though *au fait* with the latest developments in most musical styles, Charlie's own recreational listening was ever inclined towards that of those artists he'd always liked, even if some of those still alive were too old to learn new tricks. With all the virtues and a few of the faults of a virtuoso performance, 1977's *Hard Again* by Muddy Waters was a turntable fixture for a while, causing Watts to commit the heresy of preferring its overhaul of 'Mannish Boy' to the original.

Less passive pursuits than playing records were so plentiful that they precluded Charlie's desire to 'try my hand at writing more books. I enjoyed doing that one about Charlie Parker, and I've got three more up my sleeve. Trouble is finding enough time to get down to actually writing them.'[4]

He was still adding to legion credits on album covers. As the 1970s wore on, he'd be heard on a Ron Wood solo effort, *Gimme Some Neck*, and *Rough Mix* by Pete Townshend and Ronnie Lane, following the latter's withdrawal from a reconstituted Small Faces – and, for old time's sake, and with Geoff Bradford – a Brian Knight album, *A Dark Horse*.

Another assistant on the Townshend–Lane and Knight offerings was Ian Stewart, a chief catalyst in Rocket 88, a project in which he and Charlie Watts remained mainstays for as long as it didn't interfere too much with Stones matters. Essentially, however, it was the brainchild of Bob 'Big Sunflower' Hall, a boogie-woogie pianist who was, debatably, the equal of Stewart, and a friend from the G Club when the world was young. Hall had served The Groundhogs and Savoy Brown as well as making hay himself during the second wave of British blues in the late 1960s with his own eponymous group, which was of sufficient eminence to call upon such luminaries as Fleetwood Mac's Peter Green and leading British blues chanteuse Jo Ann Kelly for assistance when recording three albums for, admittedly, labels of no great commercial merit.

Hall was never short of musical activities during the 1970s either. More often than not, he'd be backing artistes engaged by a Birmingham conglomerate, Big Bear. Through its agency, 'American Blues Legends' revues came to Europe so often that a zealot in, say, Rheims or Düsseldorf would see more of the genre's Mississippi and Chicago practitioners in person than his counterpart in Laramie or Detroit had ever done – for many a blues grandee had reached the evening of his life without once appearing professionally on his native soil. A lot of them had to take time off work to trudge round Europe, guitar in hand, as did Lightnin' Slim from his Michigan metal foundry and Chicago bartender Big John Wrencher.

If the likes of Wrencher, Slim, Snooky Pryor, Good Rockin' Charles, Dr Ross ('The Harmonica Boss') and Hi-Hat Harris weren't as immortal or venerable as Muddy Waters or Howlin' Wolf, at least they were more disposed towards crossing the Atlantic to be shown respect by a hitherto-unrealised audience. Perhaps the oddest public expression of their surfacing overseas in the 1970s was a *Birmingham Evening Post* 'Pop Special' printing full-colour pin-ups of the wizened troupe of Big Bear's American Blues Legends 1973 package – heart-throbs like Homewick James, Washboard Willie and Boogie-Woogie Red. You might laugh, but two years later, sexagenarian Country Joe Pleasants scored a French chart entry with one of his Big Bear singles.

Hired to accompany Pleasants and many other of Big Bear's US imports, Pete York[5] was to take Big Bear's idea one step further by promoting and drumming in 'Blues Reunion' bands composed of white British musicians whom the blues had made more famous than it had many of the black originators. Among those old pals persuaded to take part in these events were Brian Auger, Chris Farlowe, Zoot Money and Spencer Davis.

A regular port of call was Swindon's cosy Wyvern Theatre, venue too of the first manifestation of what became Rocket 88 on 12 June 1977. 'It was originally The Bob Hall Band,' outlined the artist formerly known as Big Sunflower, 'and was formed to play a farewell concert for me when I was living and working in Swindon, and planning to move back to London. I suggested to Ian Stewart we might do a charity concert. He said, "I might know a drummer who's quite good" – and that was Charlie Watts. We got a local bass player and a brass section. We never practised at all, just went on stage and did this show.'[1]

With another pounder of barrelhouse 88s, George Green, in tow too, the repertoire was dominated by pieces by Albert Ammons, one of the most boisterous and compelling executants in the 1940s – though the idiom's optimum moment was thought generally to be a Carnegie Hall recital in 1938 featuring some of the older black masters. No one could pretend that the non-smoking Swindon bash was what it must have been like at either Carnegie Hall or in the din and nicotine clouds of the levee camps, juke joints and brothels frequented by the USA's once most shunned sub-culture. Nevertheless, there was a friendly, down-home ambience about the proceedings at the Wyvern – and another back-to-the-roots performance there in the New Year.

Both shows were taped, and edited highlights issued by Black Lion Records on an album entitled *Jamming The Boogie*, attributed to Hall and Green. That was presumed to be that until an intense discussion took place as old friendships and rivalries were renewed at Alexis Korner's 50th birthday party on 19 April 1978 in the Gatsby Room at Pinewood film studios, where London protrudes into Buckinghamshire. Guests included Dick Heckstall-Smith, Art Themen, Eric Clapton, Paul Jones – and Ian Stewart who, recalled Jones, 'wanted to get together an R&B outfit like the Ellington or Basie "small group", and he didn't want any guitarists unless they could play like Freddie Green – which meant that the only guitarist who could be in it was Alexis.'[1]

Putting deeds over debate, Stewart was behind the organisation of a show just before Christmas in the image of those at the Wyvern but relocated to Dingwall's Dance Hall in Camden Town to celebrate what he'd calculated to be half a century of boogie-woogie. The major change to the personnel was that Jack Bruce, then domiciled in Germany, was now plucking upright bass. Capitalising on qualified success as a solo attraction, he was fresh from being central figure of a looser amalgam, Jack Bruce And Friends. Passing through the ranks were players of the calibre of Mick Taylor, Larry Coryell and co-founder of The Jazz Composers Orchestra, Carla Bley, for whom Bruce sang on 1972's critically acclaimed *Escalator Over The Hill*.

Bruce's presence, as much as that of Charlie Watts and Alexis Korner – who'd become a pop star at last when singer on early 1970s hits with CCS[6] – added to the turnout at Dingwall's. Indeed, hundreds were turned away at the tail-end of a queue that stretched round the block. Many were genuine boogie-woogie enthusiasts, but quite a few had only the vaguest notion about what they were paying to hear, convincing themselves perhaps that some of that Stones, Cream and, if you like, CCS magic was going to radiate from the stage. Instead of magic, however, there was mere music played for the benefit of the musicians almost as much as the audience, even if more worthy than any produced by that boring-but-competent blues band trundling out 12-bars until chucking-out time at a pub near you.

Enough, however, lapped it up to encourage a reconvening on 12 May 1979 at the newly opened Venue, a few minutes' power-walk from Mick, Keith, Brian and Charlie's Chelsea flat of blessed memory. This time, the amalgam was billed as Rocket 88 – Ian's suggestion, and a genuflection to a 1951 Chess single by Ike Turner's Kings Of Rhythm, cited by some cultural historians as a specific harbinger of rock 'n' roll.

Next up were dates months into the future in Holland, Germany and back in Britain – notably, re-bookings at Dingwall's and the Venue – largely on the strength of the famous names promised,[7] particularly that of a delighted Watts. 'I can't keep up being a Rolling Stone all the time,' he grinned at a scribbling scribe from the *Daily Mail*, 'I like the people involved, but not the whole showbiz thing.'[8]

'If Charlie said he could do it,' agreed Bob Hall, 'we'd get major shows.'[1] They also gained an Atlantic recording contract for an in-concert album[9] taped at the Rotation, a club in Hanover, in the teeth of so-so acoustics and, by most accounts, a so-so performance.

Worse, however, was the previous evening in Hamburg. Jack Bruce often knocked back more liquor than he should have before a show, but had always got a grip on himself. Yet he'd never been as far gone as he was then. 'We were all waiting to go on stage,' remembered Bob Hall, 'and Jack was standing behind the curtain, just on the edge. Then there was this slow-motion movement of Jack and his bass falling on to the stage from behind the curtain. There was this shocked silence, but he got up and then he and Charlie – who'd also had a few – proceeded to play – separately – for the entire evening.'[1]

The road crew gazed anxiously if indulgently from the wings, but, if nothing else, Charlie, Jack and most of the rest seemed to have fun in Rocket 88 to the degree that Korner at his own expense dropped everything to fulfil a solitary booking in Britain before jetting back to an interrupted tour in his own right in Switzerland – while Watts and Stewart hurtled from a Stones studio session in Paris for Rocket 88's spot at the North Sea Jazz Festival in the Netherlands. The following afternoon, they were back in the studio, Ian's eyes bloodshot after nigh on two days at the wheel.

# 12  Return

'I often think we ought to call it a day – but I keep telling myself I'd be selfish to put my own ambitions before the needs of everyone else. I'm a Rolling Stone, and stuck with it for the present.'

*– Charlie Watts*[1]

Resident in England again, the Watts family, while maintaining the Provençal farmhouse, had found a metropolitan pied-à-terre overlooking the Thames. They were also perusing the property pages of *Country Life* for somewhere that offered privacy without imprisonment. As important as the dwelling *per se* was the space between it and the nearest neighbours. With rapidly accelerating advances in communication technology, close proximity to both storm-centres of the music business and the other Stones wasn't as crucial as it might have been before the evacuation to France – though, even in the bluster of the metropolis, who could fail to adore a homeland where female traffic wardens called you 'love', cigarettes could be bought in ten-packs, pubs were more than places where men got drunk, and *Monty Python's Flying Circus* repeats had cleared the ground for the likes of *Ripping Yarns* and *Fawlty Towers* to heave UK television from the mire of 'more tea, vicar?' sitcoms or half-hours freighted with innuendo about wogs, poofs and tit?

In deciding to return from the Côte d'Azure to his native soil, Charlie Watts was also flying in the face of the cold and rain, only three television channels, and motorways that had not thrust any tentacle into that part of North Devon where, after much deliberation, Charlie purchased a 17th-century manor house. It stood in the bucolic heart of an area where cattle grazed on the green of hills that wore halos of mist at dusk and dawn. 'England's Switzerland' was how it was described in a guide book published by the Tourist Information Centre in Barnstaple, the nearest big town to the listed building with its stone-flagged floors and exposed oak rafters.

Outbuildings in the surrounding acres included stables for the Arab horses that Shirley intended to breed, even if Charlie wasn't especially keen on any form of equestrianism. 'He got on a horse twenty years ago,' chuckled Shirley, 'and got off again almost immediately.'[2]

Eventually, the stables would house 20 ponies – and there'd be a comparable pack of dogs, among them ten border collies permitted to share the master bedroom. With some of them at his heels, 'Squire' Watts would stride forth unobserved in his gumboots on a clear, dew-sodden morning through the gardens, coppices and fields within acres spreading beneath an untroubled sky. Rather than dressing-room fug and harrowing soundchecks, the fresh air, quietude and Peace In The Valley suited one who would 'enjoy the company of dogs more than that of humans. Not that I loathe my species, but they'd find me a miserable little man after a while.'[3]

How privately ordinary the icon once worshipped from afar seemed when he and his wife became an everyday sight, unmolested by autograph hunters and worse, at fêtes, sheepdog trials and other local events where nothing much else was calculated to happen, year in, year out.

There were a few domestic hiccups – such as Charlie breaking a leg after a fall in the cellar – but he would remember this period not only for what happened at the end of it, but also for the contentment that had preceded it. During this least hectic phase of his career, who could have blamed him for, ostensibly, doing nothing in particular? Surely it was no sin to make millions out of harmless entertainment? As in the 'happy ending' of a Victorian novel, with the inheritance claimed and all the villains bested, he was well placed to settle down to a prosperous lassitude. A back-street lad who'd climbed to the top of the heap, who could begrudge him what was imagined to be a secluded but cosseted semi-retirement in his quasi-Arcadian Shangri-La?

While he actually led quite a full life outside the context of the Stones, he'd been spoken of as an old nag out to grass by those who, reacting against the distancing of the humble pop group from its audience, had applauded the now-radical *NME*'s tacit bias towards the grassroots developments of pub rock, punk, the Mod revival and whatever was on the way next. To this end, it had also lampooned 'dinosaur' acts – either over the hill like The Grateful Dead or wholesomely Americanised like a Fleetwood Mac who were as far removed from the blues band they once were as Steve Winwood would be from The Spencer Davis Group with 1980's *Arc Of A Diver*, on which more US sound laboratories received 'special thanks' than humans.

How much more gratifying it was to spend an evening in the warm, jolly atmosphere of licensed premises where the likes of Kilburn And The High Roads, Roogalator and Dr Feelgood played with more dignity and thought for the paying customer than any stadium supergroup at Wembley or Birmingham's National Exhibition Centre but otherwise forever in America, whose bass guitarist had just thrown a green room wobbler because of a misconstruing of an amenities rider in the contract about *still* rather than *fizzy* mineral water.

Though there had been places in the pub rock sun, too, for The Searchers, The Troggs, surviving personnel from Johnny Kidd's Pirates and a reconstituted Downliners Sect, it had, by definition, precluded stardom and any correlated prima donna tantrums – and so did punk after the later 1970s had come to be divided in two – pre- and post-Sex Pistols – as guitars were thrashed *allegro con fuoco* to machine-gun drumming behind some ranting johnny-one-note who behaved as if he couldn't care less whether you liked it or not. Not a week went by without the *NME* or *Sounds* howling about another new sensation ringing some changes. Somehow, most of them sounded just like The Sex Pistols.

Yet, flipping through a turn-of-the-decade edition of *Melody Maker*, the jazz and folk sections were still intact, and the Stones weren't damned necessarily with faint praise as was *de rigueur* in other periodicals. Mutual mixed feelings extended to the Stones offering financial aid when latter-day Pistol Sid Vicious was awaiting trial for murder, and Billy Doherty of The Undertones – creators of Derry's first punk release, the *Teenage Kicks* EP – proclaiming in retrospect that 'the greatest drummer of them all is Charlie Watts. He is my inspiration for playing drums. His playing swings with befitting motion which is so distinguishable. His style is dignified and impeccable. This is what makes him so unique as a player. He is the benchmark of what great drumming is all about: subtlety, creativity, style and rhythm. What he does is beatific.'[4]

What was the party line on Rocket 88? On paper, it was as artistically no-nonsense as any pub rock or punk combo. You heard fine if unambitious music – 12-bar chord changes and a four-four backbeat – played for sheer enjoyment by the ablest practitioners of the form, who were likely to be most erudite companions to a relaxing evening of discs by boogie-woogie originators – for, if nothing else, listening to Rocket 88's own output – and that of The Big Six, The Brian Setzer Orchestra, King Pleasure And The Biscuit Boys, The Big Town Playboys and further agreeably retrogressive victims of the same passion – led you back to the digitally enhanced but lower fidelity of infinitely more plausible key figures in the movement such as Cow Cow

Davenport, Cripple Clarence Lofton, Pinetop Smith and Lewis, Meade Lux rather than Lewis, Jerry Lee.

As simple keepers of the faith, however, there was no reason why Rocket 88 shouldn't have gone on indefinitely, albeit mutable in state with a turnover of personnel drawn from the same pool of faces only a telephone call away. Yet with the encroachment of dark nights of the ego and connected factors that make pop groups of whatever style or vintage what they are, it was no longer the antithesis of Charlie's 'whole showbiz thing'[5] – but perhaps it never had been in the first place. Sometimes, Mickey Waller would deputise for an indisposed Watts, and 'you'd get silly things like Jack Bruce saying he wouldn't do it unless Charlie did,' sighed a dismayed Ian Stewart. 'The horn players got fed up because Bob Hall always vamped through their solos. So everyone got fed up with each other.'[6]

Rocket 88 vanished in a haze of one-nighters *sur le continent* – where they were required sometimes to back US visitors such as Arkansas blues balladeer Jimmy Witherspoon and Country Joe Pleasants – risen anew as a jive-talkin' showman, more Lee Dorsey than Sleepy John Estes since his French chart-rider – as well as, on one occasion, Chris Farlowe for whom all signposts pointed towards the swinging '60s nostalgia trail, and being lynched if he left the stage without singing 'Out Of Time', his 1966 Number One cover from *Aftermath*.

The biggest of Rocket 88's final moments had been when German promoter Karsten Jahnke, a close friend of Alexis Korner, had shoehorned them into Woodstock In Europe, a tour on the tenth anniversary of what was still seen as the angel to Altamont's demon. Rather than less viable club dates – especially in the light of the Fatherland's accelerating economic recession – it centred on four open-air spectaculars, enthralling Cecil B De Mille-sized crowds whose enthusiasm for olde-tyme pop – which had even embraced a skiffle revival – showed no sign of slowing down.

Into the bargain, all a contracted outfit had to take with it were instruments and a pair of drumsticks, as the 'backline', megawatt PA and any keyboards required were all laid on during hours of entertainment by Country Joe And The Fish, Ritchie Havens, Arlo Guthrie, Joe Cocker, Canned Heat and other acts with at least a passing resemblance to those who'd taken the stage in the midst of the squelching mud of lakeside meadows in August 1969.

Wrinkles, baldness and belts at the last hole were the more obvious indications that individual journeys to middle life hadn't been quiet. Anyone cognisant, for example, with the grizzled Cocker's self-violated mind and body began worrying when he flagged, cheering when he rallied and glowing when a number went down particularly well. A recovering alcoholic, his hands were no longer a-tremble or his nose enpurpled, but the blue devils had not yet been sweated from him – and, before he could so much as lurch from the wings to the central microphone one evening, it was necessary for him to be sobered up with peppermint tea and Alexis Korner, who functioned as master of ceremonies as well as a cornerstone of Rocket 88.

In many respects, Korner – rather than Charlie or Jack – was the main draw for Jahnke and customers who tempered revelry with historical interest. As long ago as 1971, Hamburg had hosted a 'Tribute To Alexis' concert to mark what might have been his quarter century in the music industry – with its *Adendblatt* newspaper publishing a special poster-cum-supplement annotating his life story. To lend a series of album releases showcasing classic Chicago blues a seal of illustrious approval, he'd also been roped in by the domestic wing of the Philips record label to assist in their preparation.

Korner was to remain a huge attraction across the North Sea, while being reduced to voiceovers in television commercials back home. If also on the periphery in Britain, rock Methuselahs like Chicken Shack, Savoy Brown, Stone The Crows and Ten Years

After were likewise filling Teutonic sports stadia still – as were The Blues Band, formed by ex-members of Manfred Mann. It became convenient for Big Bear to open an office in Cologne, and Pete York to move to Munich in 1980 to commute more easily to an ever-increasing workload in a country where the popularity of the blues lingered long after the late 1960s 'boom' had subsided to distant thunder nearly everywhere else.

Though Rocket 88 was to fade away too, its impact would continue to ripple for as long as Charlie Watts remained an entertainer. The most immediate evidence of this was the use of bouncy 'Take The "A" Train', Duke Ellington's signature tune, as the introit to Rolling Stones stage appearances in the early 1980s – such as the one I attended on 25 June 1982 at Wembley Stadium, the principal UK date during another global money-spinner.

I hadn't thought of going until offered two tickets cheap by a mother of three whose husband's back was playing him up. Diving on the London train straight from a day at the mixing desk, I arrived at Paddington station in the driving rain and with Metropolitan Line trains spitefully on strike. Rather than waste money on a traffic-jammed taxi or bus fare, I decided to leg the seven miles to Wembley at Scout's Pace, ie quick-march for 20 paces than double 20 ad nauseam. Well, Jagger was a keep-fit fanatic these days, wasn't he?

He was a lot fitter than I was when I reeled up to the turnstile two hours later. All seats were taken, but I'd missed the dub-reggae and The J Geils Band, thank God. Eventually, I stood among the common herd on the pitch, while Princess Margaret and her children and all the Stones' parents luxuriated in a special compound elsewhere.

Dead on time, the main event piled on. Beyond the three chief show-offs stage front, there was Charlie, his grins less bashful and rare than of yore, whenever his eyes were teased from the drums. There was Ian Stewart, the one who'd looked too normal, finally allowed out – and old Bill Wyman, basking in the afterglow of a recent solo single in the Top Ten. He'd probably been the brains behind the delving into the past of older rockers than themselves – 'Chantilly Lace', 'Twenty Flight Rock' and the like, which were slipped in to balance recent smashes like 'Start Me Up' and the ambles down Memory Lane, spanning 20 years. Though the dark clouds and thickening twilight were more suggestive of the witching hour than Hyde Park, the mood had become lighter, friendlier since occurrences like *Satanic Majesties* and Altamont had taken them out of their depth, obliging them to concentrate on the possible.

The audience had seen it all before, but so what? The girls gasped rather than screamed when Mick took his shirt off. The music was still only one step from chaos, but the sound was crystal-clear and the Stones still rode 'em on down. During the fixed 'Satisfaction' encore, I wondered wickedly what would have happened had the main set ended with politely brief applause instead of the howling approval, foot-stomping and girls taking off their bras.

Afterwards, I joined my old mate Kevin, to whom I'd sent the other ticket. We'd been in the Boy Scouts together, and I reminded him of when he'd spent three hours pacing up and down outside a record shop in Aldershot, deliberating whether to blow three weeks' pocket money on *Aftermath*. At a wedding reception, his uncle had donned a ladies' wig and done a flawless imitation of 'that Mike Jaggers' as 'Satisfaction' shook the Dansette.

Though Kevin had since become a frozen-food executive, any pretensions of respectability evaporated temporarily through breathing the air round the Stones. Unable immediately to get out of the car park or find a pub, we shadow-boxed round the streets of Wembley, incantating 'I'm Smokin' Joe Frazier' over and over again, and asking bemused passers-by the way to the Stones concert. Driving back, we indulged in a cowardly game of slowing down to chant an adaptation of a nappy advert at gangs of skinheads. Luckily, we never stalled. Nearer the motorway, we stopped the car to take artless photographs of street furniture.

Home by 3:15am, I was back to reality. In seeing the Stones again, I'd come up for air. Though I've since resumed growing older, I'd reaffirmed my most abiding self-image that night. In the bathroom mirror at dawn, I saw not a mortgaged 33-year-old with a pregnant wife, but an 18-year-old boy, long-haired, as beautiful as a girl and as mad as a hatter.

# 13 Trouble

'During this period, I was personally in a hell of a mess.'
– *Charlie Watts* [1]

Loquacious as he often was behind closed doors, Charlie remained the Silent Stone. If not a pop hermit like Chris Curtis, Syd Barrett or Scott Walker, he didn't miss the limelight, and was relatively incommunicado in his North Devon fastness while Jagger and his then wife, Jerry Hall, were never off the pages of the more trivial tabloids. Moreover, as far as Joe Average was concerned, Watts, when asked for his opinion, was as much the group's still, small voice of reason as he'd always been, talking calm sense while the others ran around like headless chickens.

As the 1980s slipped into gear, he gave the outward impression of a person completely in command of his faculties, settling easily into middle life on the consolidated fruits of his success. The adulation, the smash hits, the money down the drain could be transformed to matters of minor importance compared to the peaceful life he felt he deserved, the domestic stability, and providing his daughter with the best of everything. In short, he seemed an affluent and happily married man, sliding into a sedate middle age in sound health and with no worries.

Actually, he was deeply worried. It never rains but it pours and, in the teeth of hearsay about a sometimes dull contentment on his country estate, virtually every aspect of Charlie's personal life was the wellspring of grave problems, not least of which was Serafina.

When he wasn't touring or shuttered in a block-booked rehearsal or studio complex, Charlie was a doting dad and, in the beginning, Serafina's upbringing had been as tranquil as her sire's job would permit – though, before she was out of nappies, she couldn't help but become aware of his wealth and celebrity.

Had they been of Paul and Linda McCartney's self-consciously homely – some might say, excessively thrifty – bent, Charlie and Shirley might have considered a nearby state secondary school for Serafina. Instead, at 14, she was packed off to Millfield, a fee-paying boarding school near Glastonbury and, though co-educational, on a par with Eton, Roedean and Harrow as an institution where the children of both old British money and *nouveau riche* studied as well as those of oil sultans and European aristocracy.[2] 'She never really came home again,' gloomed Shirley. 'I regret sending her, because at that age, it's very easy to lose touch. We had been terribly close, with Charlie away such a lot.'[3]

Into the bargain, Serafina proved a bit of a handful for her teachers, and just before the Easter holidays in 1985 she and a fellow sixth-former were to be asked to leave Millfield, allegedly for smoking cannabis. Needless to say, there was attendant – and distorted – newspaper coverage. That millions read such revelations hurt her father, especially in the light of his quoted hatred of drug abuse. Yet, as an inquisitive world was to find out, the greatest paradox during this phase of his life was that old Charlie was not only drinking quite heavily, but messing about with heroin too.

He'd been aware of this most sinister of narcotics since the late 1950s when Ginger Baker in his jazz band was soon to be a registered addict, and injecting yourself with heroin was a way of sharing something with mainlining black jazzers as disparate as Billie Holiday and Charlie Parker. This was long before pop stars and drugs became as Tweedledum to Tweedledee in lurid mid-1960s headlines, and the arrival of a new and lengthier hierarchy of 'heroes' from all phases of pop – Frankie Lymon, Keith Richards, Eric Clapton, Janis Joplin, Lou Reed, Boy George – whose credibility was enhanced by promoting a 'smack' habit necessary to both 'get high' and keep the Dracula hours of their profession. A sense of longing rather than self-hatred emanated from the addict in plain 'Heroin', a Reed composition for his Velvet Underground, and 1969's chart debut by David Bowie, 'Space Oddity', was seen in some quarters as a paean to the muck.

When the Stones resumed touring that same year, Charlie of all people knew that backstage scenes are not always as gullible fans may have imagined: a board game on the middle table, Bill tuning his bass, Ron shaving at the washbasin. Yet time that hung heavy between one concert and the next wasn't killed only with chess tournaments and tea-and-biscuits.

Up until then, not only had Charlie played no part in the sex, he had also side-stepped the hard drugs, although echoing Ovid in his *Video meliora proboque, deteriora sequor*,[4] and saying little about Keith's 'works' becoming an established if discreet part of dressing room paraphernalia during the 1970s. Heroin had come close to killing Keith – and, in 1975, had rendered Free guitarist Paul Kossoff 'technically dead' for half a minute and, a few months later, 'technically dead' to this day. In 1980, *Homecoming*, an album by folk singer Tim Hardin, was also his epitaph, preceding as it did a fatal overdose. The following April, a combination punch of liquor and heroin plus his trademark obesity had knocked Canned Heat's Bob 'The Bear' Hite into eternity too.

Taking no heed of cautionary tales and his better self, Charlie Watts embraced heroin with open eyes. 'I don't know what made me do it that late in life,' he shrugged, 'although in retrospect, I think I must have been going through some kind of mid-life crisis. I had never done any serious drugs when I was younger, but at this point in my life, I went, "Sod it. I'll do it now" – and

I was totally reckless. This phase lasted a couple of years, but it took a long time for me and my family to get over it.'[1]

His succumbing was nowhere to the same degree as Keith's, who had been obliged by law to kick it with acupuncture. Chewed up and spat out by the swinging '60s, too, Wayne Fontana, Ringo Starr, Alice Cooper, Keith Moon and Beach Boys drummer Dennis Wilson had been among many bobbing like corks on seas as shoreless. Keeping the company only of those with the same self-destructive tastes, their consumption of tranquillisers, scotch, cocaine, heroin – whatever the drug of choice – was but a temporary analgesic to the pangs of despair, and became so immoderate that the media would hint at sojourns in clinics where they were helped to confront and wrestle with their unknowable conflicts.

Thus Wayne overcame his dependence on valium and was no longer a booker's risk, while Dennis, having failed to dry out, was to drown in a Californian marina in 1983, his judgement impaired by his own tiredness and an injudicious quantity of vodka. Five years earlier, no one had been entirely surprised when the Grim Reaper had come for booze-addled Keith Moon too.

Without needing to check into any rehabilitation centre, Charlie Watts overcame heroin via his own strong will. Had he studied Latin, Seneca would have reminded him, *Pars sanitatis velle sanari fruit.*[5]

He next addressed himself to spending less time in the company of the likes of Messrs Pimm's and Johnnie Walker. One of the reasons was Shirley's increasing interest in the bottle – to the extent that she would eventually seek treatment for alcoholism: 'It was Jerry Hall who told me I should get help. I'm very fond of her. It wasn't hard to give up, but there's usually a bigger problem than the drink itself. Mine was probably caused by years and years of being married to a Rolling Stone.'[3]

Conversely, they'd see no one but each other, the estate's staff and shopkeepers for months at a time in a location where, as

Charlie admitted, 'Life would be very tricky if I didn't have a car.'[6] Furthermore, as he wasn't qualified to take any motorised vehicle on the public highway, he relied on others – usually Shirley – to take him, say, to Barnstaple, the airport in Exeter or, for the non-stop train to London, Tiverton Parkway, a station a few miles from the M5's closest encounter with the splendid isolation of England's Switzerland.

In 1983, he splashed out on a very costly 1930s Lagonda for Shirley's use, but despite this and other pretty fondnesses, Mr and Mrs Watts weren't exactly Phyllis and Corydon in Arcady – or Darby and Joan, the folks that live on the hill. Neither were they infatuated young lovers, holding hands around London clubland any more. While she looked forward to the rattle of her husband's keys at the front door that heralded one more deliverance from the treadmill of the road, she would confess, 'It's difficult for me to suddenly adapt when Charlie comes home because we do different things. It's hard for him too. He loves being at home, but after the initial enjoyment has worn off, he doesn't really know what to do. I tell him to go off and play something, but he says he's been away so much, it isn't fair – and it isn't, but what can you do?'[3]

Too soon would come another departure for a stage in another continent or weeks of work on the next Stones album, but whenever Shirley materialised at her husband's places of work, it wasn't always a joyous reunion. 'Charlie was going through a terrible time with Shirley,' observed Ron Wood. 'They were having lots of heavy arguments, and so Charlie was often late or Shirley would come into the studio and drag him out.'[7]

The mid-1980s fog of despair that shrouded the Watts household thickened when the sorrow of two deaths crossed the threshold. The first was that of Alexis Korner not long after he'd assembled a band – which included Bill Wyman and Charlie – for two evenings at the Marquee as part of its commemoration of 20 years as a going concern.

If not on the scale of Moses reappearing before the Israelites from the clouded summit of Mount Sinai – or even another Marquee night during the same season headlined by a reformed Yardbirds – Korner's return to one of the places where it had all started was such that he was as delighted as his cramped audience at being so rabidly remembered. The cheers were still ringing in Alexis's ears when Charlie Watts visited him in Westminster Hospital where he was awash with medication for recently diagnosed lung cancer. He was also plagued with unexplained pains in his head, but was insisting that he was on the mend.

In the thick of various inserted tubes and drips, he produced enough cannabis for a satisfactory smoke, and was still able to rise and strum his guitar on his room's balcony, even when death could have taken him without effort. 'What an amazing attitude,' Charlie would exclaim later. 'Not a bloody word about how ill he was.'[8]

Like riders on the Wild West frontier, it was an easy, unceremonious parting when the two old comrades went their separate ways; Charlie to the USA for an all-star gala to raise funds for ARMS (Action for Multiple Sclerosis), and Alexis to meet his maker on New Year's Day 1984 after slipping into a coma induced by a brain tumour.

The following June, the annual Nottingham Festival embraced a cancer charity night at the Royal Concert Hall in Korner's name. Among those doing their bit were Charlie, Jack Bruce, Jimmy Page, Paul Jones – and Ian Stewart, who, like Alexis at the Marquee, completed his final major concert, grinned, waved into the baying blackness and vanished into the wings.

Ian was still humping speaker cabinets and hammering the ivories when required on albums by the Stones, who always asked him first before hiring any other keyboard player.[9] Yet, while his acceptance with a crooked smile of demotion from the stage to behind-the-scenes saved him from a more mundane existence, the thwarting of Ian's ambition as a professional musician – for reasons that had nothing to do with his ability – deserves sympathy, and so does the manner of his passing in 1985.

Like Mick, Ian, if a beer-and-skittles type, had always been pragmatically concerned about personal fitness. It seemed so unfair, therefore, that a respiratory infection inflicted itself upon him as he and his family prepared for Christmas. His breathing became so laboured that he booked an appointment to see a specialist in London's Harley Street Clinic. It was during this visit on 12 December that he complained of a tightness and then shooting pains across his rib cage. Next, his heart came to a standstill in a seizure of shuddering gasps and cold sweat. Cardiopulmonary resuscitation and other procedures were applied by both the doctor and summoned paramedics, but 47-year-old Ian Stewart could not be saved.

Leaving a wife and Giles, their teenage son, the boogie man warranted obituaries in 'quality' broadsheets like the *Guardian* and *The Times*. At his send-off a week later at Randall's Park Crematorium in Leatherhead, Jeff Beck, Kenney Jones and Eric Clapton were among the famous walking behind the officiating priest. Somewhere during the prayers and eulogies was heard a tape of Ian pounding out Albert Ammons' 'Boogie Woogie Dream' and the in-person strains of those Rolling Stones still living on a well-meant 23rd Psalm. 'I'm sure Stu would have found it all quite amusing,' commented Shirley Arnold, once the group's fan club secretary. [10]

Supported by what was left of Rocket 88, the Stones performed in infinitely more orthodox fashion at an invitation-only wake for Ian at the 100 Club on 23 February, delivering a set containing little but items from the Craw Daddy before Andrew Loog Oldham's structural tampering. No ordeal of luvvie conviviality, it prompted a report in the *Daily Star* about 'the guts and energy of a teenage garage band. This was the Stones going back to their roots, playing muddy and dirty.' [11]

Last respects were to be paid on disc with the insertion of a solo piano instrumental by Stewart as an unlisted track on 1986's *Dirty Work* album, a commercial triumph born of tense 'atmospheres', murmured rancour and overt ructions. Before sessions were so much as booked, a mere attempt at discussion had driven Charlie, perhaps still trying to cope with personal desolations, over the brink. A tipsy Jagger's reference to Watts as 'my drummer' was the ignition point for an outburst of swearing and fisticuffs in a hotel's dining room, and a deft sleight of verbal judo – 'I am not your drummer! You're my singer!'[12] – prior to an ebbing away that left Charlie glowering at Mick, and Mick not daring to credit the glint in the eye of the standard-bearer of group stability.

If it hadn't been Mick, Charlie might have focused his resentment at life in general then at Keith's incurable lateness, Keith and Mick's caste-within-a-caste, Bill's passiveness or a tape operator who hummed all the bleeding time. Nevertheless, Charlie's pent-up rage ebbed, and the old brusque affection towards 'his' singer – and his guitarists and bass player – returned.[13]

The tempest dropped at home too, and Shirley at least would enter what she recognised as 'probably one of the most rewarding stages of my life after a very bad decade. I'm interested in spirituality, but have no time for organised religion. I still cling to the sentimental idea of life after death. I can't conceive of not being there, but that's such an arrogant, human way of looking at it. I sometimes wake up and think I've died, and that the thinking part of me is my spirit, which is here. It's strange. I usually wake Charlie to say, "Am I here?", and he says, "Of course you are. Don't be silly. Go back to sleep."'[3]

# 14 Swing

'I don't hate rock 'n' roll. I never said that. That's why I
don't give interviews. I haven't given one in eight years.'
– *Charlie Watts*[1]

Association with a non-melodic instrument to the rear of the
stage prejudices the acceptance of pop drummers as serious
musicians – or serious anything – by those who imagine that any
fool can bash drums. 'What I have to combat is the original
image of me as the downtrodden drummer,' moaned Ringo Starr
in acknowledgement. 'You don't know how hard it is to fight
that.'[2] Starr managed it, and his records often outsold
concurrent offerings by his former colleagues. He was also the
only ex-Beatle to make real headway as a film actor.

Other talents from behind the kit who have been up against
similar undervaluation include Thunderclap Newman's Speedy
Keen – composer of 1969 chart-topper 'Something In The Air' –
David Essex and, on the tail-end of Merseybeat, Russ Abbott,
who came into his own as a television comedian during the
1980s. More pertinent to this discussion, however, is Jim
McCarty who, despite co-writing his Yardbirds' most enduring
songs and his subsequent formation of Renaissance and lesser
known but equally innovative outfits, suffered from years of
categorisation as an incorrigible R&B swatter before recognition
in the 1980s as a colossus of New Age, the only wave of
essentially instrumental music to have reached a mass public
since jazz-rock.

Yet, as well as being pivot of Stairway, Britain's most acclaimed new age entity, McCarty also presided over an R&B combo with guitarist Anthony 'Top' Topham, who was attempting perhaps to recover scrapings of an inheritance lost in 1963 when he quit The Yardbirds for much the same reasons as Charlie Watts did Blues Incorporated. While Topham's replacement, Eric Clapton, was filling the Albert Hall for a regular few weeks every winter as the 1980s faded, The Jim McCarty–Top Topham Band could be heard for the price of a pint in the Station Tavern, within earshot of London's Westway flyover. Like Clapton, they delivered diverting entertainment that included both freshly concocted originals and overhauls of R&B set-works from another Station Tavern long ago if not especially far away.[3]

Of similar kidney was The Southside Blues Band, the surprise hit of Castle Rock '94, an outdoor event in aid of a chair lift for Saffron Walden museum – during 1994's August bank holiday. It helped that their singing guitarist's Cockney-accented continuity sparked off instant rapport with the audience. I expressed my admiration of this, and was taken aback on learning that the gentleman concerned was none other than Denis D'Ell, vocalist with The Honeycombs.

If it had little discernible effect on The Honeycombs' recorded output, Denis D'Ell was as much of a bluesman on the quiet as The Kinks, the Stones or any other denizen of the Craw Daddy and Marquee. Therefore, around the same time as the McCarty–Topham unit was in operation, he disregarded prevailing trends and put together The Southside Blues Band, mainly for engagements near his home in rural Essex, and to make a self-financed album, *Nectar*, essentially a streamlining of well-received stage favourites such as 'Louie Louie', Chuck Berry's 'Nadine' and a radical overhauling of John Mayall's 'Brown Sugar' (from 1967's *Blues Alone*).

While D'Ell and McCarty were driven to an extent by both disillusionment with the music industry and economic considerations in their respective parallel careers in 1990s manifestations of The Honeycombs and The Yardbirds, there may have been a certain psychological undertow connected to the sharpening focus of their own mortality.

Rather than go gently into that good night, many artists approaching pensionable age do not regard looking forward to the past as healthy – with much justification. Thus McCarty's premeditated rewinding to the 1960s at the Station Tavern did not milk naked nostalgia any more than, say, Jeff Beck's one-off 1993 album *Crazy Legs* – not so much a reliving of apprenticeship in a short-lived Gene Vincent And The Blue Caps soundalike outfit as a reconstruction of what it might have sounded like in a 1990s context – and David Bowie's assembly of Tin Machine, a quartet in which the 40-year-old cast himself briefly as 'just one of the guys in the band'[4] to perform what was described as 'superstar pub rock'. With an indifference towards conventional tonality, Tin Machine made a row that was at odds with Bowie's more studied solo material, causing critics to exchange nervous glances. Who'd have thought the old boy still had it in him?

To use the title of a painfully appropriate 1977 single from Jerry Lee Lewis, Charlie Watts was just as 'Middle Age Crazy' in his way as Bowie, Beck or McCarty. As well as his murky flirtation with heroin, a more positive aspect to what the amateur psychologist could ascribe to the 'male menopause' was his leadership of an ensemble that, sparing no expense, had as much relevance to hip-hop, acid house and other prevailing trends as a tract from the Flat Earth Society.

As it would be with Jeff Beck's *Crazy Legs* revisiting, The Charlie Watts Jazz Orchestra was to be sonic testimony to Albert Camus' oft-quoted, 'A man's work is nothing but this slow trek to rediscover through the detours of art those two or three great and simple images in whose presence his heart first opened.' Maybe it wasn't saying much, but he'd come closest before with

Rocket 88, albeit essentially someone else's often ragged and messy baby.[5] Also, John McLaughlin and Georgie Fame had been closer than, debatably, Charlie would ever be when the former had played alongside Miles Davis, and the latter had, in May 1967, sung with Count Basie at the Royal Albert Hall, endearing himself to the tuxedoed audience with a nervous introductory, 'Welcome to my dreams.' Fame had also dipped into his own pocket to record a 1966 LP with seasoned jazzers like Tubby Hayes, The Harry South Big Band, and Stan Tracey – a father figure of British jazz as Alexis Korner was of British R&B.

Though he acquitted himself admirably on these prestigious occasions, Georgie's income still depended on the daytime mundanities of record sales. Such a consideration didn't affect multi-millionaire Charlie Watts who, while his heart may have first opened in the poorer circumstances of his youth, now had the wherewithal to express any number of Camus' 'simple images', and thus fulfil a more pragmatic dream than Fame's or the fellow who paid a king's ransom to conduct the London Symphony Orchestra at the Albert Hall for just one night.

As it was with ramshackle Rocket 88, you wondered how Charlie's new sound venture would have fared if a tape had been offered anonymously to major record companies. It may have courted rejection, as an actual marketing experiment of this kind by Jack Bruce proved to his rueful amusement.

What if Watts and a pruned-down edition of his Orchestra – containing illuminati like Bruce – had appeared pseudonymously on a mid-week evening in a half-full jazz club near you? A disaffected onlooker's perspective might have been that, if not excitingly slipshod like Rocket 88 had been on a good night, they deserve better for their atmospheric and eminently danceable executions of 'Take The "A" Train', 'Mood Indigo', 'Cotton Club Stomp' and other genre war-horses. The most unsung hero of the night is the drummer, ministering unobtrusively to overall effect and, in his way, a virtuoso.

They're a rather specialist 'group's group' that stir up appreciation by other musicians for rigorously held standards and stylistic tenacity. Nevertheless, only by developing rather than consolidating present artistic parameters will they affirm the greater staying power that is theirs for the taking. Yeah, on the whole, they're OK, and I might catch them again next time they're in town.

Without the benefit of such objectivity, Watts and his hand-picked orchestra took a gamble on 18 November 1985 when they kicked off a week – rented by Charlie – at no less than Ronnie Scott's. Moreover, a small army of intrigued and famous hep-cats rallied round. Some of them – most conspicuously Mick, Keith and, with his funeral a month away, Ian Stewart[6] – had at least a glimmer of how much Charlie had on his plate.

He'd been confident that he'd get more than his money back from a full house for each of the seven nights on the strength of his own celebrity and that of others involved. However, aware of other chasms into which he might plunge, Watts steeled himself to face facts...but he needn't have worried. As anybody but Charlie might have predicted, an almost palpable wave of goodwill washed over him the minute he positioned himself at the kit, and the entire evening was a triumph because everyone wanted it to be.

What struck the crowd first was the sheer size of his band: 'all my favourite players, people I've admired for years'.[7] As well as comfortable old chums like Dave Green on acoustic bass and Jack Bruce – bowing a cello – there were nigh on 30 further players which, without a synthesiser in sight, included two vibraphonists, a flautist doubling on clarinet, a brass section (including four trombonists), two singers and a pianist – who was none other than 60-year-old Stan Tracey, resident at the venue for most of the 1960s, during which time he worked with Sonny Rollins, Roland Kirk and every other visiting jazz giant.

Finally, Charlie – perhaps in expanded emulation of Woody Herman's Second Herd's unprecedented three tenors and one baritone – had hired a sensational array of a dozen saxophonists – and not just any saxophonists either. Hand-picked from both veterans and up-and-coming talent, among those tearing it up that night were Evan Parker (who lived up to his talismanic surname in the heated aggression of his passagework), Alan Skidmore (arguably, the country's most adept Coltrane stylist), Peter King (co-owner of Ronnie Scott's and headliner on its inaugural night) and Courtney Pine, one of the brightest new stars in British jazz.

Charlie grinned at the salvos of clapping whenever one or other of them wrapped up a particularly bravura solo, but, as expected, he preferred not to indulge himself, choosing instead to keep smooth pace with the blowing of others. Indeed, he was flanked by two other drummers of contrasting approach: Bill Eyden – who, since The Cyril Davies All-Stars, had played for Procol Harum and, like Alan Skidmore, Georgie Fame – and John Stevens, known for being in a more abandoned People Band bag with his contemporaneous Spontaneous Music Ensemble and, in the mid-1970s, John Stevens' Away.[8]

Like many others in the ensemble, Stevens would have been equally at ease reading dots for Frank Sinatra as Frank Zappa, when supplementing his income with pot-boiling sessions. Yet everyone in The Charlie Watts Jazz Orchestra was a committed, even delighted, participant. While no one could pretend that they'd been lifted by time machine from the Cotton Club, it was great fun to make music to which you could lindy-hop and jitterbug rather than breakdance, music in a zoot suit that was nowhere to be found on the map of present-day pop, coinciding as it did with the golden age of swing, a form that, as Benny Goodman said, 'is as difficult to explain as the Mona Lisa's smile'.[9]

It was a learning experience, too, for Courtney Pine and other younger Orchestra players to dig beneath the topsoil of jazz's all-American medieval period that began in the speakeasies of 1920s Harlem and moved into the ballrooms after the repeal of Prohibition. Partly to hold at bay, however fleetingly, the realities of the Depression, it exploded across the USA and then the rest of the world by the time Hitler invaded Poland, the smug complacency of Glenn Miller came into its own, and the US record business grew into a giant concern.

The spirits less of Louis Jordan and Cab Calloway than Ellington, Krupa, Hampden, Herman, Lester Young and Artie Shaw effused from the bandstand. Benny Goodman was particularly well represented in such as a euphoric 'Moonglow' and 'Stompin' At The Savoy', with its minimal call-and-response melody line presenting a wide scope for soloing that could be simultaneously fiery and witty over accompaniment that could shift gear with the aplomb of a Formula One racer.

Though one of those Greatest Nights Anyone Could Ever Remember, the first time wasn't to be the only time, and the momentum was sustained for the rest of the week. A rebooking was arranged for the following April, and wheels set in motion for a reprise at Fulham Town Hall on 23 March 1986, as well as a short US tour, which necessitated Charlie jetting to New York to discuss details. Before the *dramatis personae* dispersed to individual activities – 'with those guys, the phone's always ringing,' sighed Charlie[7] – it was thought prudent to immortalise the show with a CD (and associated video) release, *Live At Fulham Town Hall*, remarkable for a front cover depicting just the founder of the feast's face, an old/young countenance beautified by the skill of the photographer.

Of course, Charlie's Jazz Orchestra was too expensive and cumbersome to last. Nevertheless, a 22-piece version honoured negotiated dates in the USA, commencing on 27 November 1986 at the West Hartford Music Hall, Connecticut. It focused on the east coast, culminating with two evenings at the Ritz, an art-deco palais that usually hosted rock groups. Afterwards,

Charlie – and Shirley – reserved soupçons of charm for everyone who entered their circulating orbit during après-concert refreshments. Among those to whom they doled out chat were Keith Richards and his wife – who'd flown in from his Caribbean home-from-home – and Andrew Loog Oldham who, with all his furies and hungers spent, seemed quite buoyant with rose-tinted sentiment for the old days as well as genuine pleasure at Charlie 'being exactly where he wanted to be'. [10]

The Orchestra protracted a sporadic stage career into 1987's summer with the Fulham Town Hall video on national television, the introduction of some originals and even an element of freeform into the repertoire, and appearances at the Hollywood Bowl as part of a jazz festival organised by *Playboy* magazine; back in New York at the Avery Fisher Hall, and at the Pistoia Blues Festival in Italy. Probably because he'd elected to bury himself in the thick of it rather than push himself forwards like Buddy Rich, Watts was not to figure in the annual British Jazz Awards at Birmingham's Grand Hotel. That was still the domain principally of Jack Parnell, Tony Crombie...all the old lags from the aftermath of the war. Yet personal popularity mattered little to one who was motivated by quasi-evangelical zeal not so much to further a cause but, without having to explain or intellectualise, simply being a man who'd gotta do what a man's gotta do.

Rolling Stones completists may have been almost as nonplussed by Charlie's *Live At Fulham Town Hall* as they'd been by The People Band, but for swing fans unfamiliar with the Orchestra leader's pop past, it might remain the basis of every appraisal of him.

# 15  Modern

'Light years better than anything Watts' day job has produced in fifteen years...a fabulous jazz recording.'
                                        – Option *magazine*[1]

If Charlie was disappointed about – or if he'd even heard about – the British Jazz Awards, this was mitigated in March and June 1990 when he was voted the world's best drummer in, respectively, *Rolling Stone* magazine's readers' poll and the second International Rock Awards in New York.

The Stones in general gained high positions in all relevant categories, which boded well for the forthcoming *Urban Jungle* tour of Europe, scheduled to break into East Berlin and Czechoslovakia, territories that had been *verboten* before east mingled freely with west after the Berlin Wall came down the previous November, and Checkpoint Charlie metamorphosed into a glass-towered conference centre.

These days, moving from A to B was more like a military operation than ever, requiring a staff of nearly 300 to transport the largest portable stage ever constructed – or, to be precise, *stages*. That was why some of the crew would never see the show. Even as a tape of 'Continental Drift', a track from the most recent album, *Steel Wheels*, signalled the start of the Stones' set at Rotterdam's Fejenoord arena on 21 May, 200 miles away at the Neidersachen Stadium in Hanover there were seemingly continuous errands by officials with clipboards in their hands, barked orders to humble equipment-humpers, and a general ecstasy of bustling on a half-erected edifice that had to be finished in time for the first of two nights on the 23rd.

As usual, Charlie had had a hand in its design. The dominant colours were yellow, orange and purple, and the principal image a crazed, wolf-like beast with bared fangs and claws. However, his personal caprices for this latest re-run of the ritual were subdued. T-shirted at the kit, he sported a pencil moustache and was seen to be smiling a lot more.

He had good reason. For what they'd been and for what the audience thought they had become, the group could do no wrong, especially on the dates in Glasgow, Cardiff, Newcastle, Manchester and Wembley – because we Britons like our entertainers to be survivors, and the Stones were nothing if not that. Furthermore, the country was awash with yearning for the swinging '60s. All it took, it seemed, was for a swarthy youth to remove his jeans in a launderette in a TV commercial to the lilt of Ben E King's 'Stand By Me'.

Snippet coverage in a lager advertisement on the same channel had sent a 19-year-old Hollies single to the top in 1988 – while even older mementoes either traceable to or actually by The Kinks, The Dave Clark Five, Them, The Troggs, The Spencer Davis Group, The Zombies – and The Rolling Stones – were likewise incorporated into the sloganeering, the hype and the cramming into less than a minute of everything specific merchandisers wanted to say about cars, coffee, insurance, confectionery and the like during evenings otherwise sabotaged – as they were in the late 1980s – by championship snooker. Across the Channel, too, 'Paint It Black' was back at Number One in Holland, having been employed as the theme to a TV series. Old hits had encroached on public consciousness to such a degree that time had almost stopped when one week's UK Top Ten contained only one entry that wasn't either a reissue or a revival.

Yet, unlike less fortunate brethren only too grateful that booking fees had risen temporarily through this renewed interest, the future was not the past all over again for the Stones. While *Hot Rocks*, a 'greatest hits' compilation, was in the UK album Top Ten, the fall of *Steel Wheels* from its apogee of Number Two had been reversed. Therefore, rather than milking their distinguished back catalogue, they concentrated as hard upon items from this latest offering and explorations of remote pathways – such as 1965 B-side 'Play With Fire' and 'Factory Girl', fourth track, side two, of 1968's *Beggar's Banquet* – as easy *Hot Rocks* crowd pleasers from way back when.

At times, it was just Jagger, Richards, Watts, Wyman and Wood pleasing themselves rather than their audience, seizing songs by the scruff of the neck and wringing the life out of them. As 'pure' in their field as Ravi Shankar and Pavarotti in theirs, the starkly functional guitars-bass-drums-vocals core and the thrilling margin of error remained as potent now as they had been in 1963. However, they were showbiz enough now to back-project and even line up to take a bow at the end.

For the faithful – whether there from the beginning or *Steel Wheels* latecomers – every Rolling Stones concert was a special event, particularly as the subject of the outfit's retirement from the stage was being discussed more and more. Since the mid-1970s, not a tour would pass without some twerp in the media asking, 'Could this be The Last Time?' Had this been the case after *Urban Jungle*, the in-concert *Flashpoint*, with its 12-page booklet, would have sufficed as a respectable epitaph. While you had to have been there, the most succinct description I can give of this as a listening experience per se was that The Rolling Stones sounded kind of like The Rolling Stones – and there'd never have been another like them.

The Charlie Watts Orchestra, however, had been and gone – though the eventuality of a regrouping has never been regarded as improbable, and Watts resumed his moonlighting as a jazzer with less ambitious labours of love. In summer 1992, he and Keith Richards were heard on *Weird Nightmare*, an uneven tribute album to Charlie Mingus, but of more import – if as tangential to contemporary pop as the Orchestra – was the following year's *From One Charlie To Another*, a genuflection by the newly formed Charlie Watts Quintet to Charlie 'Yardbird' Parker and, less directly, the be-bop combos that put so many of the big bands out of business.

From behind the 1957 black Gretsch kit he'd hit during the *Urban Jungle* outing, but was now more inclined to brush, Charlie presided over Peter King and David Green from the earliest Orchestra and three new – or not so new – faces. The most venerable was that of pianist Brian Lemon, a Midlander who'd rated as a rising jazz star in a *Melody Maker* poll in 1959. Largely on his recommendation, Watts had taken on trumpeter Gerard Presencer, an 18-year-old prodigy from London who, with the candour of someone in their fourth decade, was to cite Charlie as 'the best band leader I've ever worked with. He's almost quite angelic, despite going through all the stuff with The Rolling Stones.'[2]

One who went through a little of that stuff was the Quintet's *chanteur*, Bernard Fowler from New York, who'd been among the backing singers with the Stones both in the studio and on stage since the late 1980s. While he wasn't old enough to be steeped in post-war jazz traditions, he picked up the basic principles quickly and, to Charlie's satisfaction, delivered what vocals were necessary when the outfit repaired in February 1991 to West London's Lansdowne Studio – as Olympic wasn't available – to tape 'Lover Man',[3] 'Dancing In The Dark', 'Bound For New York', 'Just Friends' and further selections from Parker's catalogue for release several weeks later in the CD package that also embraced a reproduction of Charlie's long out-of-print *Ode To A High-Flying Bird*.

One of the record industry's hardiest perennials, paying homage to an influential performer over an entire album had many antecedents. Random examples are The Pupils' low-budget *A Tribute To The Rolling Stones*, *Hank Williams: The Roy Orbison Way*, *(Buddy) Holly Days* from Denny Laine, *The Zappa Album* – the late Frank's music presented in baroque style by Finland's Ensemble Ambrosius – Zappa's own hitherto-unreleased *The Rage And The Fury: The Music Of Edgard Varese*, *Ne Me Quitte Pas: Brel Songs By...* by brand leaders of English *chanson*, Gerry Marsden's *The Lennon–McCartney Songbook* – and 1988's *Sgt Pepper Knew My Father* on which several 1990s acts depped for the Lonely Hearts Club Band for a remake of The Beatles' most famous record.

The latter might be viewed as a symptom of artistic bankruptcy among newer chart contenders, content to imitate or exalt yesterday's heroes – as do further 'various artists' collections derived from the portfolios of Syd Barrett, Captain Beefheart, Peter Green and like unforgotten icons. The latest such effort germane to the Stones has been a 2003 package of six vinyl 45s by Norton, a US reissue label. These covers of numbers – some famous, most obscure – include a merely workmanlike 'Off The Hook' from our own Dartford Renegades. Yet 'Citadel' and 'Out Of Time' are delivered in baldly exciting fashion by, respectively, The Queensbury Terrors and Boston's Real Kids – who also back socialite Janet St Clair's gripping 'Ride On Baby'. Elsewhere, agreeably retrogressive enjoyment may be derived from, say, The Knaughty Knights pitching into 'Connection' and The Hentchmen making the most of 'Surprise Surprise'. Finally, the venerable ? And The Mysterions rearrange 'Empty Heart' in an attempt to improve long-faded professional matters with a credible influence.

Bereft of commercial pressure, Watts' motives for *From One Charlie...* were nowhere as suspect, but were rooted in a commitment to keeping Parker's work before the public, and to touch base somehow with the emotions that fuelled him when his adolescent self used to spin the vinyl of *Bird At St Nick's*, *April In Paris* and the like to dust.

For the music central to a recent celluloid biography of Parker, *Bird*, directed by Clint Eastwood, the alto saxophone had been isolated from the original recordings, and superimposed accompaniment, blessed with state-of-the-art fidelity, adhered as closely as jazz would allow to the notes and timbre of Kenny Clarke, Bud Powell, Dizzy Gillespie and all the rest of Parker's accompanists. The overall intention of The Charlie Watts Quintet, nevertheless, was *not* to sound just like the Parker blueprint when they gave 'em 'Perdido', 'Bluebird', 1954's 'Cool Blues' and so forth at such disparate venues as Tokyo's Spiral Hall, both the Birmingham and London branches of Ronnie Scott's and, poignantly, two electrifying engagements with guest saxophonists Alan Barnes and Julian Arguelles in June 1991 at the Blue Note in New York, where they dared to open with a slow Ellington ballad, 'Sunset And The Mockingbird', and include a Presencer original, 'Changing Reality'.

That these shows were very well received both pleased and confused Charlie: 'So many English players are world class. Yet they're not that known elsewhere. In New York, people loved them, but they never offered these guys other gigs. I don't know why.'[4]

As it had been with the Orchestra, there were frequent long gaps between bookings,[5] but ten dates in Brazil the following May with a short coast-to-coast trek across the States hot on its heels – 12 nights back at the Blue Note, then Chicago's Park West and the Palace in Los Angeles – turned the Quintet into a polished and thoroughly road-drilled unit on the crest of favourable reviews of *From One Charlie...*, and a 'live' album that belied its prosaic title, *A Tribute To Charlie Parker*, and testified to more intrinsic virtues in an industry where sales figures are arbiters of success. As expressive as the most glowing critique in the media was the reported grudging praise for *From One Charlie...* from the discerning – and dying – Frank Zappa, who 'didn't like Charlie Parker. Listening to those things, I would go, "Why do people like this?" I don't understand it.'[6]

It was a truism that the drummer's status as a Rolling Stone guaranteed the ensemble more attention than would have been warranted in the normal course of events. Where would he be otherwise? Would he still be beavering away at Charles Hobson and Gray, maybe on the board of directors by now? Perhaps he'd be running 'rhythm and improvisation' workshops at a nearby adult education centre, immersing himself in music as other family men might in do-it-yourself, photography or football. Pipe between teeth and settled in an armchair, he'd pick an album from an impressive collection and, with an observed reverence, trance out to classical music – though his soul will always be in the jazz that takes him back to a lamented youth.

In real life, cash returns for the two oblations to Charlie Parker were healthy enough for two further Quintet albums – and even a 1993 single, 'You Go To My Head' – to be considered worthwhile marketing exercises, albeit with three years between *Warm And Tender* and 1996's *Long Ago And Far Away*, on which the five were augmented by The London Metropolitan Orchestra, provoking comparisons with jazzer-turned-easy listening maestro Henry Mancini.

They had progressed from Parker to more generalised post-swing 'modern' jazz, as smooth as *Flashpoint* was rough, and hinged on a tasteful, if stubbornly North American, choice of standards, principally from the annals of the type of Hollywood movies that crop up on midweek TV during the lonely hours between the lunchtime news and the children's programmes – eg Gershwin's 'Someone To Watch Over Me' from *Young At Heart*, Sammy Cahn's 'I Should Care' from *Thrill Of A Romance* – as well as Broadway musicals ('Bewitched' from *Pal Joey*) and other ancient chestnuts, a couple of them predating 1940's first *Billboard* chart. Any one of them was crucified by Workington's answer to Tony Bennett on a beer-sodden evening in the Red Lion the other Friday.

Patiently puffing a Kool cigarette, Charlie overcame his known aversion to the dazzle of flashbulbs and the scratch of biro on notebook by showing willing at *Warm And Tender*'s press launch on 11 October 1993 at New York's Algonquin Hotel, where he deadpanned the foreseeably stupid and damned impertinent questions – many of the same ones he'd listened to in the mid-1960s – and retelling the old, old story of him and the Stones for the trillionth time while trying to steer the wry shallowness round to the Quintet.

They expected Charlie Watts to play down his own part in *Warm And Tender*. In this respect, he wasn't to play the iconoclast either, with the fewer words he'd be persuaded to utter on behalf of *Long Ago And Far Away*. Lauding the contributions of the others, especially Bernard who, he said, 'sings beautifully', he added, 'Of its type, it's a great album.'[7]

You had to admire the Quintet's boldness in recording material that less assured groups of their kind would shun – because most *Warm And Tender* and *Long Ago And Far Away* selections were disadvantaged by a head-start of up to half an embedded century of availability and airplay in 'definitive' form by Billie Holiday ('Good Morning Heartache'), Nelson Eddy ('In The Still Of The Night'),[8] Hoagy Carmichael ('I Get Along Without You Very Well'), Billy Eckstine (I'm In The Mood For Love') and, particularly, Frank Sinatra. Since then, there'd been the likes of 1970's *Sentimental Journey* by Ringo Starr-as-crooner; Diana Ross's soundtrack to her *Lady Sings The Blues* bio-pic of Holiday; a 1983 album of Carmichael by Georgie Fame in collaboration with Annie Ross, one of his smart jazz friends, plugged on a BBC2 series; and a new album of evergreens by Dr John, with Duke Ellington's 'In A Sentimental Mood' its title track.

What the hell. Like The Charlie Watts Jazz Orchestra and *Live At Fulham Town Hall*, the Quintet and its albums *had* to smoulder into form, even if whatever Charlie Watts got up to outside the context of the Stones was barely relevant in the wider scheme of things. That *Warm And Tender* and its belated follow-up were critical triumphs was neither here nor there to Charlie. It wasn't anything to do with arrogance or over-confidence about his own or his colleagues' abilities – far from it. No matter how much the pundits on broadsheet arts pages smirked at each other's cleverness, it was the bane of their existence that, thanks to the financial safety net provided by his membership of an internationally renowned pop group, someone like Charlie Watts could afford to do something that they couldn't do – and that he couldn't have cared less about their tin-pot reviews.

# 16   Bridges

'I used to practise every day. I don't any more.'
                                                    – *Charlie Watts*[1]

To get back in trim for another world tour, Charlie practised for up to ten hours a day for six weeks prior to the first rehearsal. While he continued to use the 1957 Gretsch for both the Stones and his jazz excursions, he had become to drums – particularly snares – what Lord Beaulieu was to motor vehicles. His acquisitions ranged from a tarnished kit of uncertain make from the 1920s to the gleaming splendour of a 1960 black Gretsch with an 18-inch bass drum, and a green-glitter-with-gold finish. It was just like the one Mel Lewis had played with Stan Kenton – 'but I don't think I'll ever use it,' smiled Charlie. 'It's just a lovely looking thing.'[1]

On sessions for the Stones' latest album, *Voodoo Lounge*, he'd been experimenting with instruments not generally thought of as musical – such as a metal litter bin on 'Moon Is Up' – and investigating the sonic and spatial possibilities of locations other than an isolation chamber, capturing a sepulchral echo by micing up the drums in the well of a studio's four-flight staircase.

A general reawakening of enthusiasm for recording and a return to the stage could be attributed to the long promised and amicable departure of 57-year-old Bill Wyman in 1993 after three decades. 'I wish he would have stayed,' sighed Charlie. 'Financially, he would have been a lot better off because he and I had the same sort of earnings. I miss saying hello and going to his room.'[2] Nevertheless, a change of personnel would present an opportunity to both refine known material and change stylistic habits.

After a moment's pause over the keys of their word-processors, some hacks reckoned that the most obvious candidates to replace Bill were John Entwistle and Jack Bruce, both at a loose end vocationally. The Who weren't much of a group any more, having not played together for three years. Since then, Entwistle had gone to ground on his Gloucestershire estate with slight deafness, a legacy of too many years of too many decibels. Putting his more avant-garde leanings on hold, Bruce, however, was planning to take to the road in 1994 with a 'power trio' completed by Ginger Baker and guitarist Gary Moore. Focusing principally on the USA, they'd break the ice each evening with an hour's worth of Cream favourites.[3]

A list of other possibilities was pruned down, and the final choice left to Charlie because, explained Keith Richards, 'What counts is what the drummer thinks. I said to Charlie, "You decide" – and he said, "You bastard, you put me in the hot seat!" – and I said, "Yes, for once, Charlie, once in thirty years, you're going to be the supreme judge on this."'[1]

If still in the cradle in his native Chicago when the classic Stones line-up had found each other half a world away in 1962, Darryl Jones wasn't exactly the pop equivalent of a chorus girl thrust into a sudden starring role. The main point in his favour, as far as Watts was concerned, was that he'd worked with Miles Davis (after attempting to audition over the telephone!) and Gil Evans, not to mention Herbie Hancock and BB King. Indeed, there was nothing at all to suggest that Jones wasn't the *beau ideal*. 'He's very comfortable to play with,' affirmed Charlie. 'He's very quick to pick things up, very much a rhythm section within a rhythm section. He's underneath it – which is what we need really: foundation. He's a nice man as well.'[1]

Like Charlie, Darryl would reconcile a love of jazz with working with the Stones. Like Darryl, Charlie was not self-deprecating about his love and knowledge of 1990s pop, favouring mainstream and, beneath it all, 'musicianly' acts such as Oasis: 'As daft as they can be...at least they play their instruments. Equally, I like rap rhythms'; though Watts qualified this with, 'It's great to hear, but it's such a produced thing. If you're learning to play, you never play a bass drum and a snare drum like they do on a rap record – because the tracks are altered, the sounds are altered. You can't learn to play through those. I couldn't.'[4]

But soon must come the hour when fades the fairest flower. After reaching full bloom in the mid-1990s, Britpop – which borrowed heavily from a more golden age of British beat – and the brutish sexual self-aggrandisement of rap were reduced to mere chart ballast when absorbed into the main sequence of generalised pop just like an outlying hamlet is gobbled up by an encroaching industrial conurbation. Yet the Stones still stood as strong as if their legs had taken root in floorboards, a stance that was extraordinary at a time when it was not so easy for new records by old idols to be accepted without derogatory comment by a label's quality controllers, voracious as always for new faces to exploit and discard for a fickle public.

For the Stones in the autumn of their careers, there were still *Top Of The Pops* slots – on video, mind, rather than in the chicken-necked flesh. These were inclined to adhere to a straightforward synchronisation of a musical performance rather than projecting anyone into a dramatic situation, and were shot in generally correct anticipation of one hit per album – 'Harlem Shuffle', 'Love Is Strong', 'Saint Of Me' – that tended to hover no higher than 'twixt 10 and 30. Nonetheless, they were hits all the same.

It was also business as usual on the boards. The *Voodoo Lounge* global tour – taking in maiden performances in South

Africa – was followed less than two years later by another, also attended by a million-selling album, *Bridges To Babylon*, which saw them into 1998 – or 1999, if you count the British stops at an Edinburgh rugby ground, Sheffield's Don Valley Stadium in the rain, Shepherd's Bush Empire and Wembley all postponed advisedly until after the beginning, in April, of the next tax year.

Though Charlie's shave-and-a-haircut-six-pence tom-tom introit to a reinvented 'Not Fade Away' heralded Jagger's *Voodoo Lounge* Grand Entrance for the first dates, and a section of *Bridges To Babylon* took place on a small 100 Club-esque platform in the middle of a given arena (linked to the main stage via the abrupt appearance of a mechanised bridge), the set was becoming formulaic. They'd lay on the current chart entry plus perhaps one other track from its album with a trowel, but the rest of the show would consist of the brighter flashes of past glories, some of them either dredged up for the first time in a donkey's age – with 'Route 66' the most touching of them all – or never played before outside the studio – as '2000 Light Years From Home' wasn't until 1990. For good measure, they'd chuck in an oddity too – like a revival of The Temptations' 'Can't Get Next to You' for *Voodoo Lounge*, and Bob Dylan's 'Like A Rolling Stone' for *Bridges To Babylon*.

Among the 75,000 at Wembley in 1999, Tony Hussey of *The Beat Goes On*, a mail-order mouthpiece of the swinging '60s nostalgia scene, noted that 'the individual percussion sound of Charlie Watts was never better, and when Mick introduced the musicians, the biggest applause was reserved for the shy sticksman'.[5]

Throughout the dinning weeks of this, the Stones' longest ever tour, Charlie had been as a fish beneath the merely choppy offshore waves that had superseded the stormy oceans of days gone by. The same person he'd always been, he'd found his way to the racks of Ray's Jazz Shop in Soho during an afternoon prior to one of the London spectaculars – and, during the calculated lulls in the itinerary – such as a fortnight off for 1997's Christmas and 1998's new year – he chose not to gallivant off to the West Indies like Keith or to somewhere outlandish like Mick, but to come up for air in the verdure of Devon or, less often, the sunshine of Provence, to savour as many unremarkable days as the parameters of a remarkable life would permit.

If he and Shirley were ever affected by it, they had long come to terms with 'empty nest syndrome', a common enough melancholia in middle age, after their only child had left home as well as school to edge nearer to the day when Mum and Dad become distant friends and then no more than memories.

Serafina in her mid-20s was now a painter, living in Chelsea, but she still looked homeward to the farm where her mother had established a routine of rising at 6:30am, retiring to bed 15 hours later and in between either tending to the horses or applying hammer and chisel to her latest creation. Sometimes, outlines between the two activities dissolved: 'I take my horses into the studio to stand for me,'[6] she revealed when she agreed to be the subject of one week's 'A Life In A Day', a regular page in the *Sunday Times* colour supplement, which edited a given personality's own tape-recorded words for a thumbnail sketch of both day-to-day conduct and past and present lifestyle. Charlie didn't object, even consenting to hover, hands in pockets, in the soft-focus background of the photograph of his wife that headed the piece.

It was clear to readers that, while in the enviable position of never being obliged to work again, Shirley had remained a determined self-improver. Her principal outlet for this was through her sculpture – representational with discernible structure and tangible substance – and exchanges of ideas with other locals – for, in its understated way, North Devon forged widespread and eclectic opportunities for artistic development. Along the loneliest of the district's narrow lanes, drivers will come upon an unlooked-for gallery or workshop selling sufficient calligraphy, pottery and like product peculiar to itself to keep afloat. Moreover, while Shirley didn't exhibit her work there, others of her persuasion did, in arts centres and community institutes in Barnstaple, Bideford and smaller settlements like Hartland and Great Torrington.

Mostly by word of mouth rather than through exposure in *The Sunday Times*, Shirley found buyers too, 'but I'm fortunate enough not to need to earn a living, so I don't try that hard. Charlie asked why I didn't do a bust of him, and I said, "Well, if you'd sit for me, I would." I should be more pushy and demand that he comes and sits – but, like many women, I find it hard to say, "This is what I want, and I'm going to have it."

'It's such a big house, and I'm so busy. Charlie thinks it's crazy, such hard work – but then he doesn't put much effort into anything. He's quite a laid-back person. He's around in the morning, but I don't know what he does. We usually meet up for a snack lunch.'[6]

Wholesome food had long figured in the vegetarian couple's life – though Charlie at least had acquired a comparatively exotic taste in the early days of a travelling life of snatched, irregular and unsquare meals during which it was never sure if he could masticate so much as a round of toast without having to sign an autograph or listen to starstruck drivellings. After the music was over, most restaurants that served a late-night menu were Chinese or Indian. Otherwise, his palate had been coarsened by chips-with-everything in wayside cafes. In those days, the search for a nut roast would have been fruitless anyway as vegetarianism was then an eccentricity and an inconvenience both for short-order cooks and dinner party hosts.

The Stones as a whole had never seriously considered adopting vegetarianism in the 1960s, even when they had the means to order more than beans-on-toast. On the run around the world, well-meant gourmet dishes with specious names – veal Hawaii, furst puckler, trepang soup – pampered stomachs yearning for the lardy solace of a mixed grill. You could stand them a feed at the Ritz, but they'd still be sentimental about when they used to small-talk on the pavement outside Studio 51 with The Downliners Sect, chomping newspapered cod and chips.

Charlie had been the first Stone to at least try a meat-free diet – though, even when he lived in London, he was an irregular, even non-, eater of, say, the brown rice and vegetables that cost half a crown (12½p) at Notting Hall Gate's Macrobiotic Restaurant, patronised by so many of a particular type of diner that it provoked raids by the Scotland Yard drugs squad and its sniffer dogs, and led the proprietors to insist that all guests sign a written statement that they were not in possession of 'controlled substances'.

Other pop stars were also sufficiently hip to understand that, like, cruelty to animals is wrong, but, after a few weeks of patronising trendy restaurants that had 'gone macrobiotic', the smell of frying bacon would trigger a backsliding. Charlie and Shirley, however, were strong-minded enough to stick with vegetarianism in their various country retreats where they could gaze at lambs gambolling round their mothers in a meadow as the collies protected the flock from more innocent predators than humankind. However, they weren't evangelical about it like Paul McCartney, whose first wife, Linda, had been the founder of a multi-national vegetarian food company with an award-winning range of products stocked in supermarkets in Barnstaple where Kim, the Watts' housekeeper, pushed a trolley from aisle to aisle, working her way through Shirley's grocery list.

'I don't know why I didn't have a housekeeper years ago,' wondered Shirley. 'Actually I do: Charlie didn't want anyone around. Yet he spends half his day chatting to Kim.'[6] Some household chores he undertook himself, among them washing antique crockery by hand for fear that a machine would discolour and scratch its veneer.

Now and then, he would accompany either Shirley or Kim to the shops and be all-but-unnoticed in undisguised anonymity, browsing in a second-hand book store, studying a poster for August's Bude Jazz Festival or scouring the street for any emporium bearing the sign 'junk' or 'bric-a-brac' that might contain a desired collector's item in a heap of scratched LPs.

'That was one of them Rolling Stones, you know', someone might whisper after he'd knocked back a pint in some far-flung village pub or watched with interest a cricket match on its green. Watts might not have been as keen on the sport as Jagger or Wyman, but he too had rubbed shoulders with professionals like Ian Botham and Mike Gatting, and was a reader of match results on the Internet, even in the throes of a Stones world tour.

The pop squirearchy had also started taking up pastimes recommended by those born into privilege. For example, Steve Winwood, born in a Birmingham semi and owner since 1970 of a pile not far from the ancestral seat of the Mitfords, had an open invitation to take part in the disgusting aristocratic passion of stag hunting.

Huntin', shootin' and fishin' didn't appeal to Charlie – very much the opposite, in fact – but he was, apparently, now so actively involved in the region's sheepdog trials that he was a recognised authority. Yet for all his fingers in this and other bucolic pies, a few bars of Ellington, Parker or Davis, either on the stereo or Jazz FM, would invoke a frisson of delight and transport him, however temporarily, from the country quiet. 'I still have the same childish enthusiasm for those people as I had then,' he would confess,[2] about to embark on another episode – the most unusual thus far – of highly practical evidence of his devotion.

# 17 Project

'Nobody ever buys these things, but they're lovely to do, and they give me a chance to play in a totally different way to how I do in the Stones.'

– *Charlie Watts*[1]

Since Gene Pitney, Phil Spector and, purportedly, members of The Hollies assisted on 'Not Fade Away' and the debut LP in 1964, further catalytic cronies and guest players were wheeled in over the decades to add icing to all manner of Stones cakes. The outside parties of greatest eminence were, I suppose, John Lennon and Paul McCartney with their backing harmonies on 1967's 'We Love You'.

Respected more for what he did than how famous he was, Jim Keltner had added idiosyncratic patterns of percussion to the *Bridges To Babylon* tracks after the beat had been invested by Charlie in Hollywood's Ocean Studios. Jim had become a Clem Cattini – or, more to the point, a Hal Blaine – *du jour*, with first refusal on all Los Angeles record dates, despite corner-cutting 'progress' from the late 1970s when Japanese boffins invented a drum machine that, within the strictures of perfect time-keeping, would make a deliberate mistake within bar lines – perhaps fluffing a floor-tom fill – every now and then in order to preserve some vestige of humanity. Other electronic drum devices – notably Linn – made no such allowances, however, to the degree that, in Britain, 'There are too few flesh-and-blood musicians nowadays,' lamented Clem Cattini. 'The session scene is defunct as far as I'm concerned.'[2]

None the less, like Eric, his sound engineer brother, Jim Keltner in the States learnt the button-pushing new idioms, and was able to programme a Linn with such accuracy that, unlike the rap patterns that had baffled Watts, nothing appeared too impossible an accomplishment for any competent studio drummer. Keltner had also educated himself in the use of sequencers and sampling, a technique that began plaguing pop in the mid-1990s[3] as the 'twanging plank' bass sound had in the 1980s.

Jim had come a long way since being Friends with Delaney and Bonnie. He'd been introduced as 'the greatest drummer in the world' by the very leader of Ringo Starr's All-Starr Band, a troupe formed in 1989 to join the likes of The Beach Boys, The Who and The Monkees on the nostalgia trail. Years earlier, the sharp-eyed had also spotted Jim smacking the skins alongside Ringo in George Harrison's celebrated *Concert For Bangladesh* spectacular at Madison Square Garden.

Never short of studio as well as stage work since, he presided over a casual combo of other session shellbacks simply to let off steam after tapping out take after take of someone else's music in the drum booths of LA. Christened 'Attitudes', not so humble were the aspirations of the group when Dark Horse, a label founded by George Harrison in 1974, underwrote and issued two of its albums and a pestilence of singles – the third of which, 'Sweet Summer Music', actually crept into the Hot 100.

In 1988, Keltner was hired by George to assist on *Volume One* by The Traveling Wilburys, a 'supergroup' consisting of himself, Bob Dylan, Roy Orbison, Jeff Lynne – once creative pivot of The Electric Light Orchestra – and Dylan's then guitarist, Tom Petty. Described by Harrison as 'skiffle for the nineties',[4] its do-it-yourself air was reflected in minor experiments, such as Keltner's whacking a refrigerator's wire grille with brushes.

He brought a far greater abundance of such ideas to *The Charlie Watts–Jim Keltner Project*, an album of two years' gestation that began during the recording of *Bridges To Babylon*, as illustrated by the presence here and there of Keith Richards and, on keyboards, Mick Jagger. While those two had been head to head at the control panel, mulling over what to add to the raw backing to, say, 'Saint Of Me', the Stones' drummer and Keltner ensconced themselves in another studio in the same complex.

'We were mucking about,' explained Charlie, 'and Jim brought in some song sequences he made from sampled sounds, and asked me to play over them. He's been sampling stuff for years, household items, metal objects, pipes, all sorts of organic things, and we started to jam over them together. Jim's such a tasteful player. He never over-hits, but he can be very tricky. The thing with drums and percussion is that the overtones, after a while, become little melodies in themselves.'[5]

After a while, the two were using every minute they were not required for *Bridges To Babylon* to work on what had become a more constructive collaboration than merely 'mucking about'. If not potentially remunerative, it was, they decided, too intriguing to just amuse Keith, Mick and anyone else within earshot of the grooves and rhythms that effused from their tiers of processed sound. 'The percussion and the various electronic things make the music here,' Charlie would tell them, 'and that was kind of the interest because I'm not normally into that. I'm not playing any differently from anything I've ever done. Jim's parts are very techno sequences. It was very exciting, very interesting. I don't know if I'd ever choose to do it again either.'[6]

Flesh was layered on to the Hollywood skeleton when Watts flew 20 boxes of tapes and floppy disks over to Twin Studios in Paris for moulding into items of sharper definition for release on a nine-track CD. As he wasn't as sufficiently schooled in the aural possibilities of state-of-the-art equipment, Watts received practical instruction *in situ* from Philippe Chauveau, a French drummer, who earned a credit with Charlie as the album's co-producer.

Much depended, too, on the proficiency of the other instrumentalists. Given this brief, Chauveau had picked and chosen violinist Marek Czerwiaski, bass guitarist Remy Vignolo, pianist Emmanuel Sourdeix and others whose names are as obscure now as they were then in English-speaking territories, but they were the finest Paris could offer, and Charlie did not presume to dictate notes and nuances to them or the players of a pot-pourri of melodic exotica including a *berimbau*, a *cuica* and a Moroccan *souk*.

He delegated much of the technological donkeywork, furthermore, to Chauveau because, 'Jim told me I needed a computer editing system called Pro Tools. It's another world to me. I thought, "What are they talking about?", but I found Philippe and we used some great Parisian jazz and world music musicians he knew. Then we started chopping and editing the tracks, and I sent them back across the Atlantic for Jim to hear.'[5]

There would be parts of *Project* that he'd have changed had he not been busy with the Stones and other matters, but some sections had been assembled literally second by second and, belying any private anxieties about his console skills during the repeated re-running of each taped mile, the engineers were impressed by the visitor's learned suggestions about amplitude, stereo placement, degeneration and suchlike, though correct terminology might have deferred sometimes to wordless vocal expressions like snatches of a Dada poem.

'I don't know how to judge the record really,' Watts intimated when he'd finished. 'I just find I like it, but I don't know why. It's kind of uncharted territory, but I'd like to think of it as sounding tomorrow rather than yesterday.'[6]

Without listening to it, but recognising his name on the light-khaki front cover, some record retailers filed *The Charlie*

*Watts–Jim Keltner Project* under 'Rolling Stones' – as they once had *Brian Jones Presents The Pipes Of Pan At Joujouka* – or, less frequently, 'jazz'. 'It probably won't appeal to jazz fans,' Charlie contradicted. 'It's a mish-mash kind of thing. I'd love people to like it as a dance record.'[5]

He wasn't being facetious. During a resurgence of unadulterated psychedelia in the 1980s, disco rhythms were married to synthesiser *arpeggio*, instrumental meanderings, perfunctory and abstract lyrics, and evidence of painstaking investigation of *Satanic Majesties*-period Stones, early Pink Floyd and Jimi Hendrix as well as The Soft Machine, Hawkwind, Caravan, Magma, Gong, Van Der Graaf Generator and others of the same kidney.

In the bowels of Reading's Paradise, the Fridge in Brixton and Deptford's Crypt, this 'head music for the feet' was oddly familiar to those aged hippies snapping their fingers within, if not to the majority of attendees who'd been little more than psychedelic twinkles in their fathers' eyes during the Summer of Love. As it had been in 1967, strobes flickered and ectoplasmic *son et lumière* was projected on to the walls as the bands played on and on and on for cavorters with eyes like catherine wheels. Modern trimmings included programmed accelerations of tempo as the night progressed and, consequently, more dancing than trancing.

The polyrhythms of *The Charlie Watts–Jim Keltner Project* certainly induced a near-trance-like effect in me, but it wasn't intended to 'go nowhere' like Brian Jones' Joujouka music or a lot of Jim McCarty's new age stuff. It was more akin to 'acid jazz', which was the outcome after the 'new psychedelia' was fused with revived interest in modern jazz – and so was ambient jazz, ambient techno, ambient pop, hardcore, acid house, hip-hip, trip-hop, jungle, ragga and further sub-divisions.

You had to be sharp to spot the shades of difference, and the likes of me tended to lump all of them together as 'the modern dance' after it surfaced in mainstream pop through the chartbusting efforts of The Art Of Noise, Prodigy, The Shamen, The Orb and Enigma. While it is tempting to rationalise the modern dance as bearing the same parallel as punk had to stadium rock, it was undercut with far greater respect for pop's elder statesmen. British multi-media team Coldcut, for instance, was flattered when asked to remix an old smash by Blondie, while Peter Green was featured in a remake of his Fleetwood Mac's 'Albatross' by Chris Coco, Brighton club disc jockey and mainstay of Coco-Steel-and-Lovebomb, an amalgam of 'acid house' persuasion – though the new 'Albatross' was more ambient techno.

Then, in 1995, there was Screaming Lord Sutch's 'I'm Still Raving', another assisted exposition of the modern dance that 'at over 140 BPM [beats per minute]', it says here, 'really "kicks" and will get any club moving'. The following year, Eric Clapton – as 'X-sample' – had a go at trip-hop with producer and keyboard player Simon Climie, issuing a 'bland, colourless album',[7] *Retail Therapy*, as 'TDF'.

Martin 'Youth' Glover, a respected modern dance producer, was the enabler of Paul McCartney groping his way through a first and foremost essay as a modern dance exponent, albeit hiding themselves beneath a pseudonym – The Firemen – but a fusion of 'down-tempo house' and a vague strata of dub reggae was heard on 1994's *Strawberries Oceans Ships Forest*, and ambient techno on 1998's *Rushes* – though good old-fashioned guitars reared up among the synthesisers and samples, and the overall effect was considered tame and old-fashioned by Youth fans.

All the same, a qualified contemporary prominence for *The Charlie Watts–Jim Keltner Project* wouldn't have been out of the question, even less so if they'd selected and edited a track for a single. If this had led John Citizen to seek out the album, he could possibly have at least half-liked it if he enjoyed, say, Enigma – who fused Gregorian chant with the modern dance – and Astralasia's 'Sul-E-Stomp', which starts almost as a traditional Irish reel before an abrupt segue into a section of more typical new psychedelia fare, ratifying their Swordfish's comment that, 'There tends to be a mixture of all sorts of culture within our music. We might throw something from Australia in with something from India and try and cross all the cultures over. It's never directed at one vein.'

As such, Watts and Keltner's offering also had much in common with – but was in only the most superficial artistic debt to – Brian Eno and David Byrne's pioneering *My Life In The Bush Of Ghosts* from way back in 1981 – a superimposing over rhythms drawn from African tribal sources of whispers of melody, and field recordings of a radio evangelist, Muslim prayers and Egyptian pop music among others.

To like resonance, Jagger's cinematic string synthesiser dominates the framing of Keltner reading – through a megaphone – quotes from Tony Williams – with something about the ride cymbal being the centre of the universe among one of the few discernible lines (yielding a similar effect to that of Jimi Hendrix's mumbling of 'You'll never hear surf music again' on his Experience's quasi-instrumental 'Third Stone From The Sun'). Keltner's text wasn't self-created, but from a drumming magazine's eulogy for the Lifetime leader, who'd just died at the age of 52. 'It was meant as a sort of requiem,' elucidated Charlie.[5]

Actually titled 'Tony Williams', it had precipitated the naming of each of nearly all the other items after a North American jazz drummer admired by both – 'Max Roach', 'Shelly Manne', 'Art Blakey', 'Kenny Clarke' and so forth. 'If this project had come about in London,' reckoned Watts, 'I'm sure it would have been "Phil Seaman", "Tony Oxley", "John Stevens" and the others.'[4] Nevertheless, like abstract impressionism in modern art, the purpose was for every piece not to illustrate the sound and style of its subject – records took care of that – but to convey an essence of him in some non-specific way, perhaps for reasons you couldn't articulate – or, in Charlie's words, 'It's not anything to do with them as players. It's more the feeling I get from just watching them play or hearing their records. It's in honour of them.'[5] Significantly, not a note of Gillespie-esque trumpet or Coltrane-like saxophone was to be heard.

Therefore, if too 'clever' for the commonweal, *Project* cannot be dismissed as an exercise in non-melodic intellectualism, a victory of technique over instinct. For Watts, Keltner and others of their vintage, perhaps it blended a sense of nostalgia within the actuality of passing time, but the inner visions evoked by the album vary from person to person and are guided by the mood of the hour. Without referring to the track listing, I let the music envelope me in its paranormal and fragmented array of samba, 'industrial', Nigerian 'high life', disco, Missa Luba mass, muzak, jungle and what defies succinct description. There's even a sub-flavouring of mid-1960s Stones in there too (on 'Max Roach') as well as a breath of the Orient – via violin rather than 'Paint It Black' sitar – in 'Kenny Clarke'. 'He lived in Paris for a while,' disclosed Watts. 'They make a lot of Arabic records there with unpronounceable names, and I play a lot of them at home. I just knew the sound I wanted.'[5]

Even with a couple of the numbers beyond the ten-minute mark, it didn't induce restlessness in me, though I flagged a little during the remixes – on a limited-edition bonus CD – by Restless Soul, Coldcut and other multi-media teams, but perhaps I should heed Charlie's advice: 'When the remix guys get hold of it, you can't be precious. You've got to forget it. If they don't like it, they'll wipe it and do another bit.'[5]

# 18   Classic

'If I didn't get nervous, it wouldn't be right. I get scared if
I'm playing in a pub to two drunks in a corner with a
piano player. The drums scare the life out of me.'
                                              – *Charlie Watts*[1]


Charlie and Jim never did become the toast of the modern dance
scene. In retrospect, their album had less to do with the
discotheque than modern classical because, though aspects of it
might have aggravated the argument of arch-minimalists Steve
Reich and Philip Glass, that the very notion of machine-music was
unnatural and 'creepy', *The Charlie Watts–Jim Keltner Project*
may be seen as a minor and belated catalyst in the dissolving of
outlines between highbrow and lowbrow, pop, classical and jazz.

During pop's fleeting 'classical' period when *Sgt Pepper's
Lonely Hearts Club Band*, *Their Satanic Majesties Request* and
their ilk had ushered in concept albums, rock operas and other
questionable 'works', CBS had promoted Reich and fellow
minimalist Terry Riley as if they were rock stars, while Apple
had stumbled upon tall, long-haired John Tavener – 'discovered',
purportedly, by Ringo Starr of all people – as some sort of
English equivalent, and Island had seen similar potential in
'Samurai of Sound' Stomu Yamash'ta, a percussion virtuoso
awarded a Classical Grammy for an album of pieces by Henze
and Maxwell Davies.

These two composers, as well as Cage, Berio, Stockhausen,
Varese and other giants of 20th-century classical music, were

as likely as anything from the Top 40 to blast from the car stereos of the thinking pop musician then. 'Revolution 9', a tape collage reminiscent of Cage on a 1968 Beatles double LP, reached a far wider audience than Cage's *Fontana Mix* and all its lesser avant-garde antecedents combined – antecedents of which most of its buyers were unaware. Furthermore, Varese in particular infiltrated jazz, as exemplified by a siren intruding upon the drum solo on the title track of The Roland Kirk Quartet's *Rip, Rig And Panic* ('inspired by the music of Edgar [*sic*] Varese'). [2]

This effect had been lifted from 1933's *Ionisation*, a *l'art pour l'art* opus that still trips most easily off the tongue whenever Varese is discussed by the sort of people who, though claiming not to be especially musical, would buy automatically a ticket for a town hall classical concert. Certainly, *Ionisation* overshadows still far worthier Varese compositions, and was the closest he ever came to spreading beyond the intellectual fringe.

Some applaud the cool nerve of a piece consisting of just percussion – though it wasn't the first. In seeking to boil down music to its rawest state, Varese – like Cage – had recognised that primitive people relied on nothing but percussion for instruments. Moreover, such limited and acoustic resources still fed the imagination of those untroubled by the dos and don'ts that traditionally affect creative flow. Random examples are Malayan 'ketimum' or 'water splash' music (hydro-percussion), Buddhist monks chanting to accompaniment from *kei*, *taiko*, *hachi*, *nyo* and other beating implements, and any number of drum solos in jazz.

In 1930, Amateo Roldan, conductor of the Havana Philharmonic Orchestra, composed *Ritmicas V* and *Ritmicas VI*, the first formalised works for an all-percussion ensemble. The world might have been the talented Roldan's oyster, but then unfashionable Cuba was enormous enough for him. He was also a half-caste...and, in the 1930s, that was just about that.

Bearing the same relationship to Roldan's folky *Ritmicases* as dairy butter to low-fat margarine, *Ionisation* – a scientific term for chemical decomposition by electricity – strictly speaking, wasn't quite 'for percussion only'. While it was written for an assortment of unpitched instruments – including anvils – there were parts too for a 'high' and a 'low' siren and, for the final 17 bars, glockenspiel, bells and piano during 14 unequal 'episodes', or rhythm collages, created by instruments – some constructed especially – and individual timbres detailed with cheese-paring exactitude.

On paper at least, it sounds not dissimilar to tracks on *The Charlie Watts–Jim Keltner Project*, which, had it created more of a stir, might have been worthy of staging as, what had been in swinging '60s parlance, a 'happening'. Perhaps it could have been staged at the Roundhouse, in a recital room at Carnegie Hall or elsewhere that presented concerts in which the artistic concepts were generally more intriguing than the executions, and the highlight of the evening for some was the opportunity to chatter in licensed premises later about how 'interesting' it all was – rather akin, in fact, to the aftermath of a People Band recital so long ago.

'If the demand came,' nodded Charlie, 'I might get it together and do it like a Philip Glass concert I once saw in New York. I'd have Philippe programming on one side, and Jim and I in the middle, mucking about with some guests – but the only thing I wouldn't want to happen is for people to think that because these tracks are named after these great drummers, I'm going to play like them.'[3]

Arrangements of two items from the Keltner collaboration were to be integrated into the set after Watts formed a new jazz outfit – a ten-piece – and tracks were sometimes loud and clear over the sound system when the hordes were waiting to see the Stones in person on this world tour or that one-off performance – though a seven-figure amount for just one little

Stones show on the eve of the millennium in New York couldn't drag Charlie away from what he had planned to do in his West Country haven. As distant fireworks exploded in a night sky untroubled by neon, he smiled at how little the money on offer had meant to him.

By shielding himself as far as he was able from the music business and the inevitable publicity it attracts, Watts and his family still walk around the towns on the estuaries of the Taw and the Torridge without inviting much comment. Serafina was back again, having returned from Bermuda, where she had moved with her lawyer husband Nick and Charlotte, their baby daughter. She found that the situation wasn't to her liking, and, after three years in the colony, had gone home to mother – and father, who, in 2001, had stuck his head above the parapet by consenting to be a 'castaway' on *Desert Island Discs*, a BBC Radio 4 series almost as long-running as *The Archers*, that 'everyday story of country folk', the omnibus edition of which preceded *Desert Island Discs* on Sunday mornings.

The eight records he picked to while away his imaginary years as a Robinson Crusoe were, predictably, mostly from the jazz age – though he also included a clip from a 1960 *Hancock's Half Hour*, cricket commentator John Arlott discussing bowler Jim Laker, Vaughan Williams' transcendental *Lark Ascending* and an excerpt from a Stravinsky ballet.[4]

His choices punctuated a dialogue in which, prompted by questions from presenter Sue Lawley, he telescoped his life. If you compare his saga to that of Jagger, you'll arrive at the precise disparity between the drummer at the back and the show-off lead singer: Mick was to be knighted by the Prince of Wales, and Charlie was acclaimed as the country's eighth best-dressed man by *GQ* magazine in June 2001; Mick's production company was responsible for *Enigma*, one of the year's most heavily plugged movies, while Charlie fended off overtures about a cameo in Channel 4 Mafia drama *The Sopranos*; Mick starred in a 2001 television special to boost sales of his latest solo album, but, with no current release to promote, The Charlie Watts Tentet commenced a fortnight at Ronnie Scott's that June.

Striking a balance between the unwieldy Orchestra and the limitations of the Quintet, Watts had selected personnel from both, plus newcomers like South American percussionist Luis Jardim and, on vibraphone, Anthony Kerr. The line-up varied only slightly as most were happy to let other ventures, such as the faithful David Green's own Trio, take care of themselves in order to play with Charlie at home – and abroad in autumn with a one-nighter in Barcelona and residencies at the respective Blue Note clubs in Tokyo and New York, where the band leader, if no Bob Monkhouse, proved a proficient if laconic interlocutor, developing quite a polished patter. In New York, he gave a particularly good account of himself when responding to backchat from Keith Richards, seated with his retinue near the front on the first evening.

As the tension built on the opening night at Ronnie Scott's, Watts might not have minded swapping the unsettling hush for the uproar on the 1960s 'scream circuit' with just Keith, Brian, Bill and Mick. 'I hate that silence,' he shuddered, 'when they come to listen. I hope people talk. It's got good acoustics. You can hear everything – so it's more exposed for me than being on one of those bloody great big stages in front of ninety thousand. I don't play that loud, even with the Stones, so they mic you pretty closely.'[1]

He was, therefore, glad of Richards' phoney insults at the Blue Note, and this with Charlie's own disarming wit made for a hugely entertaining evening that included the expected Parker, Ellington and Miles Davis preferences, along with a solitary vocal performance, courtesy of Luis Joachim, of Dizzy Gillespie's 'Tin Tin Deo'. The set concluded with an encore of 'Take The "A" Train', a number that, while he didn't risk being lynched if he omitted it, had become to Charlie and his jazz groups as 'Jumpin' Jack Flash' to the Stones.

'The only difference between us and Westminster Abbey,' smiled Charlie, 'is we don't do weddings and coronations.'[5] As one of the leading contributors to the rich tapestry of Britain's performing arts, the Stones were leading an even more fulfilling life as cultural ambassadors – as demonstrated by a concert debut in Moscow. 2001 closed with the group as the realm's seventh highest-earning pop act – down from fourth the previous year, and behind Pink Floyd, Dido, Enya and the works of The Beatles, but ahead of David Bowie, The Bee Gees, Robbie Williams, Atomic Kitten and a more recent teen sensation, Hear'Say.

When the Stones re-entered the top five of this tabulation by touring again in 2003, a lot may have seemed outwardly different – what with all that high-tech – for anyone who'd mortgaged three months of takeaway meals for admission to an act that, apart from the golden oldies, he hadn't heard much since 1983's 'Undercover Of The Night', the last single that, without logical blindness or retiming of the truth, could be described as a big hit.

To insiders, however, everything was the same. 'It's a repetition of what I've been doing for forty years,' averred Charlie. 'There's a minor flow of adrenaline going through my veins, but that's about it.'[6] As usual, he was in his chosen stage outfit maybe three hours before each appearance. Minutes before showtime, Ron Wood and Keith might be missing still, but, flanked by their retainers, they'd excuse a pedantic and tardy arrival with a joke as Watts jabbed at his watch, not raring to go exactly, but 'dragged into the excitement. I don't actually get excited myself. I always get very nervous when they're filming – because you can play a song two hundred times – which we usually do – and the one night they choose to film the bloody thing, you muck it up.'[6]

Of deeper historical interest than footage of the latest tour was 2003's *According To The Rolling Stones*,[7] a corporate autobiography in the form of transcripts of taped reminiscences plus a discography, a treasury of photographs, a chronology and lengthy reflections by Giorgio Gomelsky, photographer David Bailey and other carefully selected friends and fellow travellers. Bill Wyman, for whom no piece of information about the group had been too insignificant to be without value, would have volunteered to be what was designated its 'consulting editor'. However, since he was no longer a Stone, all fingers pointed to Charlie who, apart from that silly heroin episode, had been closest to the centurion at Pompeii who'd kept his head while all those around him were losing theirs.

Naturally, it was a best-seller; its high retail price mitigated by a weight comparable to that of a small paving slab. As for the content, it didn't consist so much of unfamiliar anecdotes and new twists to the plot as snippets of detail that the most obsessed fan – and Bill Wyman – wouldn't find totally fascinating. Adding to what was known already were estimations of motive, weighing of experience and the old yarns recounted in the subjects' own words, albeit with a turn-of-the-century retrospection that is influenced by the fact of being observed, and no anchoring narrative for that Tibetan monk who still hasn't heard of them.

Just as serious a fault was its lack of perspectives from living dramatis personae of more relevance to the story than Sheryl Crow (support act on the last two tours), some novelist from Florida or a professor of music at York University. Where were Dick Taylor, Mick Taylor, Wyman, Oldham...? But where do you draw the line? Glyn Johns? Carlo Little? Bobbie Korner? Art Themen? David Green? By including all the acts on the same labels? Everyone who ever covered a Stones song? The foresters who felled the trees to make the paper on which they were written?

*According To The Rolling Stones* was still, however, a likeable and courageous account – and a thought-provoking companion to this one. It also passed the litmus test of any pop life story in that it prompted a compulsion to rise from the armchair to put on the records. Finally, while the swinging '60s and its endless fallout are hardly the Schleswig-Holstein question – the most complex affair ever to perplex European politics – the Stones tome, despite an unavoidable subjectiveness, was certainly a more palatable way to at least scratch the surface of what the fuss was about than a thousand Open University treatises.

Yet *According To The Rolling Stones* hasn't been the last word on a tale that, like the painting of the Forth Bridge, will have no ending (any more than that of The Beatles, still an active market force more than 30 years after their disbandment). Nevertheless, for anybody who derives deep and lasting pleasure from studying raw data about producers, engineers, dates, locations, composing credits and chart placings, I'd recommend Martin Elliott's *The Rolling Stones: Complete Recording Sessions*,[8] the standard reference work on every official and bootleg recording, issued and otherwise, on which the Stones together so much as breathed – though this will need updating as, following the last tour, the group has spent another eternity in the studio.

Perhaps a snowballing of events since 2003 will necessitate further editions of *According To The Rolling Stones* with Charlie at the helm again, but I suspect that uppermost in his mind will be a book-length analysis of drummers and drumming that has, apparently, been several years in gestation, although, he says, 'I haven't got past thinking about it yet. I got the idea from a cricket book, *101 Favourite Batsmen* – or was it *Bowlers*?'[3]

None the less, regardless of whether he's been rocking back and forth, red-eyed and unshaven, in front of a late-night word-processor, trying to think of anything constructive to say about Dave Clark, Watts has been as vocal in his capacity as one of the official patrons trying to save Stoke Newington's Vortex Jazz Bar from closure[9] as he'd been in the 1980s on behalf of a similarly threatened Ronnie Scott's.

His very pragmatic support of jazz over the decades was rewarded when a dream came true in summer 2001, when Charlie recorded with Chico Hamilton, the 'first guy that I ever heard on record that made me want to play the drums'.[1] Not only that, but Hamilton composed a number in Watts' honour for the album (entitled *Forestorn*). Clocking in at less than a minute and a half, 'Here Comes Charlie Now' wasn't much of a song – or, as its subject admitted, 'not quite Stravinsky sitting on the edge of the Baltic, writing about the sea',[1] but that was beside the point.

# Epilogue
## Indweller

'Charlie says the fame means nothing to him because he
doesn't need his ego massaging – but I've seen him when
he goes to take his bow on stage. I know he likes it.'

*– Shirley Watts* [1]

Charlie Watts had arrived at the gateway of the new millennium
with a fortune secured less by the Stones' latest output than the
now tightly controlled repackagings of music recorded decades
earlier when Number Ones were almost a matter of course. Yet
if he'd stuck with Blues Incorporated or semi-professional Blues
By Six to the bitter end, it's likely that he'd have recouped little
more than memories – not all of them golden.

During a Stones spectacular at Wembley Stadium in the
1990s, Carlo Little would be operating a hot-dog trailer
outside. As the onions were being fried in readiness for the surge
afterwards, what was he thinking as Pavlov's dog-type
explosions of acclamation punctuated every segment of muffled
megawatt noise measured out by the beat of the drummer
who'd gone the distance with the Stones instead? What if King
Harold had won the Battle of Hastings? What if Adolf Hitler
had been strangled at birth? What if Mick Jagger had been
cross-eyed?

Carlo was still living in the Wembley area then, happily
married and owner of what might be described in estate agency
parlance as an 'ideally situated' house. [2] Yet, to quote one of the
late Screaming Lord Sutch's more doleful witticisms, 'if he hadn't

scribbled down Charlie's phone number for Brian Jones, Carlo could have bought the entire estate'.

On the third anniversary of Sutch's apparent suicide in 1999, Little organised what a handbill described as 'an evening of remembrance' beginning with 'quiet reflection' at the graveside at Pinner New Cemetery at 6pm. This was followed by a rather shambling show at the Ace Cafe by a bill that included The Downliners Sect and former Artwood Art Wood, Ron's older brother, both from the old days of the Moist Hoist, three-in-the-morning word games at the Korners, the smell of oil paint and turpentine, beehive hairdos, Georgio Gomelsky, 'I Got My Mojo Working', The Cyril Davies All-Stars at Harrow-on-the-Hill, and what Charlie Watts said to Art Themen at the Troubadour in 1962.

Anecdotes about the Stones aren't always affectionate, but no one has a bad word to say about Charlie, either as a person or a musician. The lad himself, however, was often quite denigrating about himself. 'I don't really like much of what I've done,' had been one comparatively recent and over-generalising self-criticism.[3] As for the Stones, he'd bitten the hand that was feeding him with, 'We're a terrible band really, but we are the oldest. That's some sort of distinction, isn't it – especially in this country. That's our claim to fame, you know. Carry on, lads, regardless!'[4]

Yet, if he had not been so fully occupied with 'the greatest rock 'n' roll band in the world', Watts might have won a place in British cultural history as a jazz virtuoso for reasons that have nothing to do with flamboyance or mean display. Like the attire of the most elegant gentleman – like his own attire – Charlie Watts' purpose was to be inconspicuous, though missed if not there, within the ranks of his Orchestra, Quintet and Tentet, and even The People Band. Matured like a good wine, a talent far above the ordinary dwelt within the limits of a self-imposed stylistic puritanism.

A similar understated orderliness is the hallmark of his other life as an easy-going country squire where, concluded Shirley, 'We never go out, never. We like being on our own.'[1] She said it with neither malcontented sarcasm nor insular pride, but as a statement of plain fact.

# Notes

In addition to my own correspondence and interviews, I have used the following sources, which I would like to credit:

## Prologue: Onlooker

1  *Sunday Times*, 2 August 2003.
2  *Q*, October 1989.

## Chapter 1: Drums

1  *Guardian*, 16 January 2004.
2  *Rhythm*, June 2001.
3  *Rolling Stones '76* (magazine, Second Foundation, 1976).
4  *The Rolling Stones: The First Twenty Years* by D Dalton (Thames & Hudson, 1981).
5  *The Oxford School Music Book* (OUP, 1951).
6  A name that attempted to express verbally its basic rhythm.
7  *The Big Beat* by M Weinberg (Billboard, 1991).
8  *Best Of Guitar Player*, November 1994.
9  Rather than play in an orthodox swing style, Clarke kept the beat principally on the ride cymbal rather than the bass drum.
10  Brubeck's 'Unsquare Dance', a UK Top 20 entry in 1962, was used in a 2004 ITV commercial for the Nationwide building society.
11  *Downbeat*, February 1987.
12  The kit used by jazz and the first rock 'n' roll drummers was a standard dance band set-up which, by the mid-1950s, was bass drum and pedal (right foot), small tom-tom (mounted on bass drum), floor tom (right hand) snare drum for the off-beat (right hand), two cymbals ('crash' – for sudden accentuation – and 'ride' – for continuous playing) mounted on stands. To the left, the hi-hats (two cymbals facing each other) are brought together with a snap by a left foot pedal to provide a 'matching' but more unobtrusive

off-beat to the snare. Later, the hi-hat stand was heightened to be within easy reach of the stick. The drum shells were usually of wood.

## Chapter 2: Art

1   *Rolling Stones In Their Own Words* ed. D Dalton and M Farren (Omnibus, 1980).

2   *The Rolling Stones: The First Twenty Years* by D Dalton (Thames & Hudson, 1981).

3   *Acker Bilk* by G Williams (Mayfair, 1962).

4   As exemplified by Aaron 'T-Bone' Walker, a major post-*bellum* blues voice, whose full-throated singing and terse guitar passagework were to be echoed by Chuck Berry. By the late 1940s, swing-styled arrangements for trumpet and tenor sax were accompanying Walker's grippingly personal blues shouting and rapid single-note fretboard improvisations.

5   *Rhythm*, June 2001.

6   *Beat Merchants* by A Clayson (Blandford, 1995).

7   *The Big Beat* by M Weinberg (Billboard, 1991).

8   *Best Of Guitar Player*, November 1994.

## Chapter 3: Blues

1   *Rolling Stones '76* (Second Foundation, 1976).

2   Other famous former Harrow School of Art students include Vivienne Westwood, daughter of a local sub-post office's proprietors. She left after a term to train as a teacher. Her boyfriend, Malcolm McLaren, future *éminence grise* of punk and, later, a chart entrant in his own right, also studied at Harrow. Westwood was to become an elder stateswoman of British fashion design, and was decorated by the Queen in 1992.

3   *Downbeat*, February 1987.

4   *Alexis Korner: The Biography* by H Shapiro (Bloomsbury, 1996).

5   *The Rolling Stones: The First Twenty Years* by D Dalton (Thames & Hudson, 1981).

6   *Rhythm*, June 2001.

## Chapter 4: Stones

1   *The Rolling Stones: The First Twenty Years* by D Dalton (Thames & Hudson, 1981).

2   *Alexis Korner: The Biography* by H Shapiro (Bloomsbury, 1996).

3   *Rolling Stones '76* (Second Foundation, 1976).

4   Today, he is a surgeon at the Royal Berkshire Hospital in Reading.

5   Which would still be hosting 'an evening with the blues' in 1966.

6   *Melody Maker*, 19 July 1962.

7   *The Big Beat* by M Weinberg (Billboard, 1991).

8   *The Rolling Stones Chronicle* by M Bonanno (Plexus, 1995).

9   *Best Of Guitar Player*, November 1994.

10  *Rolling Stones In Their Own Words* ed. D Dalton and M Farren (Omnibus, 1980).

11  *Keith Richards In His Own Words* ed. M St Michaels (Omnibus, 1994).

12  *The Drum Book* by G Nicholls (Balafon, 1997).

13  *Rhythm*, June 2001.

## Chapter 5: Beat

1   *The Rolling Stones: The Greatest Rock 'N' Roll Band In The World* ed. D Dalton (Star, 1975).

2   *Rolling Stones In Their Own Words* ed. D Dalton and M Farren (Omnibus, 1980).

3   *Rhythm*, June 2001.

4   *Downbeat*, February 1987.

5   Charlie Watts and Bill Wyman were to accompany Bo Diddley on an edition of *Saturday Club* prior to his return to the USA. A revival of 'Bo Diddley' by Buddy Holly – albeit recorded before his death in 1959 – had reached Number Four in the UK charts the previous summer.

6   *Reading Chronicle*, 1 May 2002.

7   *Keith Richards In His Own Words* ed. M St Michaels (Omnibus, 1994).

8   *Sunday Times*, 10 August 2002.

9   Because Watts couldn't be contacted in Gibraltar about a booking at the Invicta Ballroom in Chatham on 15 March 1964, Mickey Waller, then one of Marty Wilde's Wildcats, drummed for the Stones that night.

## Chapter 6: Silence

1   *The Big Beat* by M Weinberg (Billboard, 1991).

2   *Teenbeat Annual* (World Distributors, 1964).

3   *Melody Maker*, 2 November 1971.

4   At the suggestion of actress Susan Hampshire, they became The China Plates in 1966.

5   *Beat Merchants* by A Clayson (Blandford, 1995).

6   *Beat Instrumental*, February 1966.

7   *New Musical Express*, 22 January 1965.

8   *Downbeat*, February 1987.

9   *Rolling Stones A–Z* by S Weiner and L Howard (Grove, 1983).

10  *Love Me Do* by M Braun (Penguin, 1964).

11  Paris press conference transcript, 20 October 1964.

## Chapter 7: Marriage

1   *Melody Maker*, 5 April 1966.

2   *Pop Weekly Annual 1966* (World Distributors, 1965).

3   *Rolling Stones In Their Own Words* ed. D Dalton and M Farren (Omnibus, 1980).

4   *Boyfriend Book 1966* (City Magazines, 1965).

5   *Mojo*, September 2003.

6   *The Big Beat* by M Weinberg (Billboard, 1991).

7   *Downbeat*, February 1987.

8   There were erroneous claims that Clark did not drum on his own records, though he was a competent enough instrumentalist on stage.

9   *Midland Beat*, No. 32, May 1966.

10  *Melody Maker*, 12 April 1975.

11  Exemplified most obviously by Charlie's lone two-bar breaks in '(I Can't Get No) Satisfaction'.

12  *Melody Maker*, 14 May 1966.

13  *Travelling Man: On The Road With The Searchers* by F Allen (Aureus, 1999).

14  *New Musical Express*, 4 March 1966.

15  Quoted in *Beat Merchants* by A Clayson (Blandford, 1995).

16  *The Rolling Stone Interviews Volume One* (Straight Arrow, 1967).

17  *Only The Lonely* by A Clayson (Sanctuary, 1998).

## Chapter 8: Houses

1   *Rolling Stones A–Z* by S Weiner and L Howard (Grove, 1983).

2   *Rolling Stones In Their Own Words* ed. D Dalton and M Farren (Omnibus, 1980).

3   *Disc*, 22 March 1969.

4   Roy C Smith of accountants Comins & Son Ltd, who were employed by The Rolling Stones (*Q*, March 1989).

5   *Sunday Times*, 10 August 2003.

6   *Mojo*, September 2003.

7   Following his later incarceration for matricide, he was the subject of 'The Ballad Of James Gordon' by British country-rock star Terry Clarke.

8   *Melody Maker*, 16 May 1970.

9   Also known as 'The Red Rooster'.

10  More calculated – and accurate – would be Charlie's deviation from the orthodox eight quavers in a bar on the hi-hat on 'Brown Sugar', the next Stones 45. 'Charlie misses out the second beat of the bar on the hi-hat,' notes Alan Barwise, 'raising his right hand to let the left hand land. It's an amazing

shuffling feel that I've never heard any other drummer play. It certainly can't be reproduced on a machine.'

11 *World Wide Dave Clark Fan Club Newsletter* No. 58, December 1984.

12 *The Big Beat* by M Weinberg (Billboard, 1991).

## Chapter 9: Jamming

1 The People Band's eponymous album was released by Transatlantic. The group were to have a cameo – as 'The Krakow Jazz Ensemble' – in the 1987 movie *Stormy Monday*, written and directed by Mike Figgis.

2 *Zigzag*, No. 40, Vol. 4, issue 3 (undated).

3 *Rhythm*, June 2001.

4 *Rolling Stones In Their Own Words* ed. D Dalton and M Farren (Omnibus, 1980).

5 *Rock's Wild Things: The Troggs Files* by A Clayson and J Ryan (Helter Skelter, 2000).

6 *Best Of Guitar Player*, November 1994.

## Chapter 10: Exile

1 *The Rolling Stones: The Last Tour* by J Karnbach (Sidgwick & Jackson, 1983).

2 *Rolling Stones In Their Own Words* ed. D Dalton and M Farren (Omnibus, 1980).

3 Fascinated by the occult, and prone to bouts of dependency on hard drugs, Bond was heading for a personal and professional low. On 8 May 1974, he either slipped or was overcome by an urge to end it all, and died under the wheels of a tube train at Finsbury Park underground station.

4 *Maximum Led Zeppelin*, spoken-word CD biography (Chrome Dreams ABCD101, 2001).

5 *Rhythm*, June 2001.

6 *Sunday Times*, 3 November 1991.

## Chapter 11: Boogie

1 *Alexis Korner: The Biography* by H Shapiro (Bloomsbury, 1996).

2 *Rolling Stones In Their Own Words* ed. D Dalton and M Farren (Omnibus, 1980).

3 *Shattered*, Issue 20, 26 November 2000.

4 *Rolling Stones '76* (Second Foundation, 1976).

5 York replaced the long-serving Graham Burbridge in Chris Barber's Jazz and Blues Band in 1977.

6 CCS – Cosmic Consciousness Society – was a big band whose arrangement of Led Zeppelin's 'Whole Lotta Love' became the best-remembered theme tune to *Top Of The Pops*.

7   Among later members was Cincinnati-born guitarist Danny Adler of two London-based groups, The De Luxe Blues Band and Roogalator. Charlie Watts drummed on the third De Luxe Blues Band album, which was produced by Ian Stewart.

8   *Daily Mail*, 25 June 1980.

9   Entitled *Rocket 88*, it was produced by Stewart, and its sleeve was designed by Watts.

## Chapter 12: Return

1   *The Rolling Stones Chronicle* by M Bonanno (Plexus, 1995).

2   *Sunday Times*, 3 November 1991.

3   *Sunday Times*, 2 November 2003.

4   *Rhythm*, June 2001.

5   *Daily Mail*, 25 June 1980.

6   *Blues In Britain* by B Brunning (Blandford, 1995).

## Chapter 13: Trouble

1   *Sunday Times*, 17 August 2003

2   One of Serafina's younger contemporaries at Millfield was Sophie Dahl, a model who was later to be linked romantically with Mick Jagger.

3   *Sunday Times*, 3 November 1991.

4   'I see and approve of better things, but accept the worse that I condemn.'

5   'The desire to be cured is the first step towards health.'

6   *Rolling Stones In Their Own Words* ed. D Dalton and M Farren (Omnibus, 1980).

7   *According To The Rolling Stones* by M Jagger, K Richards, C Watts and R Wood (Weidenfeld & Nicolson, 2003).

8   *Alexis Korner: The Biography* by H Shapiro (Bloomsbury, 1996).

9   Most recently, Jerry Lee Lewis, who, apparently, had turned down an invitation to play on 1983's *Undercover*.

10  *The Rolling Stones Chronicle* by M Bonanno (Plexus, 1995).

11  *Daily Star*, 25 February 1986.

12  *The Rolling Stones: Complete Recording Sessions* by M Elliott (Cherry Red, 2002).

13  Charlie was to be godfather to Mick's daughter, Georgia May, born in 1992.

## Chapter 14: Swing

1   *Rolling Stones In Their Own Words* ed. D Dalton and M Farren (Omnibus, 1985).

2   *The Wit And Wisdom Of Rock And Roll* ed. M Jukubowski (Unwin, 1983).

3  After Topham quit in 1990, the group continued as a trio.

4  *Rock: The Rough Guide* ed. J Buckley and M Ellingham (Rough Guides, 1996).

5  When I was driving through Barnstaple late one afternoon in summer 1989, I noticed that an act called Jamming With Edward was billed to perform in a town-centre bar. As I was late for one of my own engagements further west, I didn't have time to investigate whether this had anything to do with Charlie Watts.

6  Bill Wyman was to attend later in the week.

7  *Downbeat*, February 1987.

8  Apparently, Watts had also approached Ginger Baker to join the Orchestra.

9  *The Swing Book* by D Penner (Back Bay, 1999).

10 *2Stoned* by A Oldham (Vintage, 2003).

## Chapter 15: Modern

1  *Option*, October 1992.

2  www.kenmat.dircon.co.uk/presencer.html

3  By coincidence, a wartime standard that was more in the air than actually popular in the early 1990s. It was, for instance, recorded with no lyrical alterations by Germany's Udo Lindenberg to reflect what he called his 'flexible' sexuality.

4  *Record Collector*, No. 253, September 2000.

5  Following a long lay-off, the Quintet played at the 100 Club as recently as February 2001.

6  *Guitar Player* (special Zappa edition), May 1994.

7  *Rhythm*, June 2001.

8  Composed by Cole Porter in 1937 – and nothing to do with The Five Satins' opus of the same title in 1956.

## Chapter 16: Bridges

1  *Best Of Guitar Player*, November 1994.

2  *Mojo*, September 2003.

3  Five years later, Bruce was to hit the nostalgia trail more openly by replacing none other than John Entwistle in Ringo Starr's All-Starr Band.

4  *Rhythm*, June 2001.

5  *The Beat Goes On*, July 1999.

6  *Sunday Times*, 3 November 1991.

## Chapter 17: Project

1  *Rhythm*, June 2001.

2   *Record Collector*, No. 211, March 1997.

3   I succumbed myself when a tape of an air-raid siren plus a vari-speeding of the stamping bit in The Dave Clark Five's 'Bits And Pieces' were undercurrents of my 1998 arrangement of Jacques Brel's 'Next (Au Suivant)', one of my contributions to *Ne Me Quitte Pas; Brel Songs By...* (Irregular IRR033, 1998).

4   *Kaleidoscope* (BBC Radio 4), 30 November 1987.

5   *Record Collector*, No. 253, September 2000.

6   *Shattered*, Issue 19, 20 June 2000.

7   *All-Music Guide To Electronica* ed. V Bogdonov, C Woodstra, S Erlewine and J Bush (Backbeat, 2001).

## Chapter 18: Classic

1   *Rhythm*, June 2001.

2   Sleeve notes to *Rip, Rig And Panic* by The Roland Kirk Quartet (Mercury 220 119 LMY, 1966).

3   *Record Collector*, No. 253, September 2000).

4   Charlie's record selections in detail were Duke Ellington's 'Jack The Bear', 'The Way You Look Tonight' sung by Fred Astaire, Charlie Parker's 'Out Of Nowhere', 'Night And Day' by Frank Sinatra, Stravinsky's 'Dance Of The Coachmen And Grooms' (from the fourth movement of *Petrouchka*), dialogue between Tony Hancock and Sidney James in 'The Reunion Party', John Arlott on Jim Laker, and Vaughan Williams' 'Lark Ascending'.

5   *Rolling Stones In Their Own Words* ed. D Dalton and M Farren (Omnibus, 1980).

6   *Sunday Times*, 2 November 2003.

7   *According To The Rolling Stones* by M Jagger, K Richards, C Watts and R Wood (Weidenfeld & Nicolson, 2003).

8   *The Rolling Stones: Complete Recording Sessions* by M Elliott (Cherry Red, 2002).

9   Once a month since 1994, the Vortex has hosted Pirate Jenny's – named after a character in Brecht and Weill's *Threepenny Opera* – and has been the most pivotal venue to nudge English *chanson* from haphazard cells of activity into cohesion.

## Epilogue: Indweller

1   *Sunday Times*, 3 November 1991.

2   Through Charlie, Carlo and his wife, Iris, received tickets for a Stones show in Paris – that included access to the VIP area. They also attended Mick Jagger's birthday party that July.

3   *Best Of Guitar Player*, November 1994.

4   *Rolling Stones In Their Own Words* ed. D Dalton and M Farren (Omnibus, 1980).

# Index